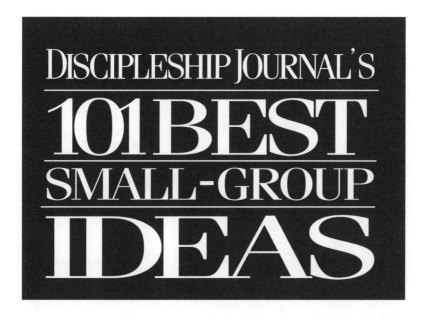

DISCIPLESHIP JOURNAL'S
101 BEST
SMALL-GROUP
IDEAS

COMPILED BY DEENA DAVIS

NAVPRESS
BRINGING TRUTH TO LIFE
NavPress Publishing Group
P.O. Box 35001, Colorado Springs, Colorado 80935

OUR GUARANTEE TO YOU

We believe so strongly in the message of our books that we are making this quality guarantee to you. If for any reason you are disappointed with the content of this book, return the title page to us with your name and address and we will refund to you the list price of the book. To help us serve you better, please briefly describe why you were disappointed. Mail your refund request to: NavPress, P.O. Box 35002, Colorado Springs, CO 80935.

The Navigators is an international Christian organization. Our mission is to reach, disciple, and equip people to know Christ and to make Him known through successive generations. We envision multitudes of diverse people in the United States and every other nation who have a passionate love for Christ, live a lifestyle of sharing Christ's love, and multiply spiritual laborers among those without Christ.

NavPress is the publishing ministry of The Navigators. NavPress publications help believers learn biblical truth and apply what they learn to their lives and ministries. Our mission is to stimulate spiritual formation among our readers.

Cover illustration: Elizabeth Brandt

"How to Prepare and Do a Word Study" is taken from *Using the Bible in Groups,* by Roberta Hestenes. © 1983 by Roberta Hestenes. Used by permission of Westminster Press.
"How to Write Bible Study Material" is used with permission of *Leadership.*
"Worship in Small Groups" is taken from *Sixty-Nine Ways to Start a Study Group* by Larry Richards. © 1973 by The Zondervan Corporation. Used by permission of Zondervan Publishing House.
"How to Promote Fellowship in Your Group" is taken from *How to Be a Christian and Still Enjoy Life.* © 1989 Gospel Light. Used with permission.
"Help for the Homeless" is used by permission of *Leadership.*
"Eight Ways to Serve Your Local School" is adapted with permission of *Worldwide Challenge* magazine. © 1994 Campus Crusade for Christ, Inc. All rights reserved.

All Scripture quotations in this publication are taken from *The Living Bible* (TLB), © 1971 owned by assignment by the Illinois Regional Bank N.A. (as trustee), used by permission of Tyndale House Publishers, Inc., Wheaton, IL 60189.

Printed in the United States of America

6 7 8 9 10 11 12 13 14 15 16 / 06 05 04 03 02

Contents

Prayer

Fellowship

Evangelism

Serving

Missions

PART ONE

SMALL-GROUP LEADERS

Best Ways to Plant, Water, and Grow Healthy Small Groups

1
Before You Lead

A small-group leader tells how preparation, illustrations, and group dynamics can be used in leading small-group Bible studies.

Preparing for the Study

When we consider Jesus' example, His lifelong reverence for God's Word is evident. Matthew 5:19 demonstrates this and suggests the attitude I need to have toward the Word of God: "Anyone who breaks one of the least of these commandments and teaches others to do the same will be called least in the kingdom of heaven."

Respect for God's Word governs a careful preparation for the groups I lead. I do a thorough study of each lesson or topic. Then I pray through the Scriptures covered in that particular study. Finally, I pray through the Scriptures for the members of the group.

This preparation gives me confidence to communicate the content. I find that the more prepared I am, the less I talk. Ideally, I'm there to guide the discussion, not to dominate it.

In preparing each lesson, I develop a simple objective that states what truth(s) I'd like the group to discover. I write the discussion questions with the answers in different colors, and I record any illustrations that help teach or communicate the idea.

These are my permanent study guides. I keep them together in a notebook. When I want to lead a study I've led before, I pull out the study guide, revise it where necessary, pray through it, and it's ready to be used as effectively as the first time.

Illustrations

Small-group settings allow for a variety of teaching approaches. I use illustrations to clarify and communicate ideas.

Jesus used illustrations freely. Watching events around Him supplied Him with an abundance of material for teaching life principles to His followers. Mark 12:41-44 records Jesus' stationing Himself to watch people contribute to the treasury. When the poor widow dropped her two copper coins into the slot, her example became an on-the-spot illustration for the disciples to learn the spirit behind giving. I strive to be observant in everyday situations and apply those situations to our study.

Group Dynamics
I use group dynamics so that the whole group will participate. I define a group dynamic as any activity that personally involves all the group members. I'm convinced that the use of group dynamics increases understanding, retention, involvement, and enjoyment in the Bible study. A question/answer discussion is a highly structured group dynamic. Other dynamics include role plays, debates, and skits.
—*Becky Brodin, Minneapolis, Minnesota*

2
Setting Goals

Three key components of small groups can work together to keep your group on track: (1) clearly articulated objectives; (2) Scripture that supports and refreshes those objectives; and (3) questions that help you evaluate your success. Here is how one small-group leader sets up his goals.

Objectives
1. To relate ourselves to Christ and His plan for our lives.
2. To develop a close, honest relationship with others.
3. To create a spiritual climate in the areas where we live.
4. To create an impact in the world through specific service to others.

Scripture
■ Luke 11:10, John 15:5, Acts 17:28, Ephesians 3:17.
■ Matthew 18:20, Acts 2:42, Ephesians 4:2-3, James 5:16.
■ Matthew 5:13-16, Acts 1:8, 1 Corinthians 13:4-7, Ephesians 5:1, Colossians 3:10-15.
■ Matthew 20:26-28, 25:35-36; Luke 10:2; John 21:15-17; James 2:17.

Questions
■ Are we seeking the mind of Christ in our lives?
■ Are we a joy to live with?
■ Are we salty enough to make another person thirsty?
■ Are we part of the solution?

—*From* Training Manual for Small Group Leaders, *by Chaplain Robert Black, Space Command Community Chapel, Peterson AFB, Colorado Springs, Colorado*

3
Qualities of a Good Opening Activity

Finding the right activities to start out your small-group meeting is important. But choosing opening activities that work well is often difficult.

A good activity prepares and propels the group into the meeting. Here are some guidelines to help you choose and incorporate successful activities into your meetings.

1. Make sure the activity starts on time.
2. The activity should be enjoyable. It should produce a high level of energy and motivation in the group.
3. The activity should invite the group members into the group. It should have a warm and friendly tone.
4. The directions for the activity should be clear to everyone. Describe them or post them in the room.
5. Be sure to indicate how much time the activity will take. Will it be open-ended or will there be a time limit?
6. The activity should be well organized. It should move smoothly from one phase to the next.
7. The activity should direct the group's focus toward the content to be covered in the main part of the meeting.
8. The activity should include every person in the group.
9. The activity should encourage and facilitate group interaction. Every member should have a significant amount of interaction with at least one other person in the group.
10. An activity that involves problem solving or an opportunity to expand the group's awareness or knowledge will be the most effective.
11. The activity should serve as a transition for the group members. It should help them leave their pre-group activities behind and concentrate on the group's task ahead.

—Navigator staff

4
Writing Your Own Bible Studies

Though small groups are becoming part of a growing number of churches, few pastors and church leaders receive training on how to develop small-group materials. You've probably used material that doesn't spark good discussion or that takes away the fun of discovery by spelling out everything.

Maybe it's time to develop some of your own studies. I've found two key rules for writing studies: Never tell when you can ask, and know your audience.

Never Tell When You Can Ask

When I'm writing a study I use a method I call "thinking backward."

First, I decide what I want people to know, feel, and do by the end of the study. I might even write a number of statements down, such as: "By the end of this study I want people to know what to do when they feel anxious. I want them to identify any anxiety they're experiencing now and share it with the group. I want them to apply Philippians 4:6-7 by praying for their needs in the group."

Second, I think of questions to guide the discussion toward these objectives. Once in a while I need to explain certain points. But always I ask myself, "Is it necessary to write this out, or is there some question I can ask to lead people to say it themselves?"

Know Your Audience

Knowing your audience involves more than knowing names, ages, and occupations. You'll come up with great ideas for your study if you think about your audience's lifestyle and needs:

■ Why are they participating in this study? What do they want to get out of it?
■ How well do they know the Bible? What do they already know about this subject?
■ What challenges are they facing right now?
■ What do they do in their spare time?
■ Is this a subject they are interested in? Is there some aspect of it that would spark their interest more?

■ What is happening in our culture that relates to the subject? How could it be worked into the study?

This information will help you in three ways. First, *it will help you determine a proper balance between learning biblical content and personal sharing.* Most people say they join small groups primarily to develop relationships with other Christians. But they want to grow in their faith as well.

Second, *it will help you develop application questions specifically geared to felt needs.* Let's return to my fictional study on Philippians 4:6-7. If I were writing different versions of this study to use in youth groups, singles' studies, and marrieds' groups, I would insert specific questions for each group. Questions for a group of married couples in their thirties might include:

■ What pressures, due to raising young children, do you face in a typical week?
■ How well do you handle those pressures?
■ At what time of day do you feel the most pressure?
■ How have these pressures affected your marriage?

Third, *it will help you add variety and creativity to your studies.* Creative openings to your studies—I call them "warm ups"—will encourage people to talk.

Finally, conduct an occasional survey to see what your group thinks about the studies they've gone through. You may be humbled by some of the results, but you'll learn which studies are on target and which ones are missing the mark.

—David Boehi, a writer for the Family Ministry of Campus Crusade for Christ

5
Identifying Types of Questions

Most leaders are familiar with the question sequence used in inductive Bible study: observation questions first, interpretation questions second, and application questions last. To be proficient with the inductive method, however, you should be able to identify each of these types of questions.

A keen ability to recognize the kind of questions going around in discussion will help you predict and guide the direction of the discussion.

An informational question is another name for an observation question; an analytical question is an interpretation question; and a personal question is an application question. Below are the distinctive characteristics of each type.

One: INFORMATIONAL QUESTIONS

An informational question requires the learner to remember specific facts in order to answer the question: What are the actual words of the Bible passage? When did this event take place? Who was involved in the story?

Informational questions allow everyone to begin on common ground and provide a proper launching point. For example, suppose your group is studying the Book of Job and the lesson aim is to determine how the Book of Job's view of suffering differs from our own. Informational questions might be "How does Elihu explain suffering?" "Who proposes the view that suffering is punishment for sin?"

Two: ANALYTICAL QUESTIONS

Analytical questions encourage students to attach meaning to the facts, thereby developing concrete concepts or principles: What is the meaning of this parable? What meaning did its author intend? What motivated this character to act the way he did?

Examples of analytical questions might be: "Why is suffering a problem for Job?" "How does Job see the relationship between sin and God?" "Does Job's view of suffering change?"

Three: PERSONAL QUESTIONS

Personal questions seek out a learner's values and attitudes and reflect them in the light of what that person has discovered in the Bible: "How does this information fit in with your own facts, beliefs, and values?" "Is this your view of the world?" "What action or behavior has become necessary for you?"

The focus of these questions is to guide learners in their own decision making and values forming. Examples might be: "Do you find Job admirable? Why, or why not?" "What would you have said to Job? Why?" "Do you feel any obligation toward others who are suffering? Why?" "Which of Job's sufferings would be hardest for you to bear? Why?" "Do you know anyone who is suffering? What could you do to help alleviate that suffering?"

On Your Own
Following is a list of questions, developed for Philippians 2:5-11. Practice your identification skills by deciding whether each question is an informational question, an analytical question, or a personal question. Notice the key words that appear in each kind of question.

1. In what areas of your life do you find it most difficult to act selflessly?
2. What does it mean to say that Christ "emptied Himself"?
3. Why did Christ condescend as described in verses 6-8?
4. Whose attitude are we to adopt?
5. How will God's human creation ultimately respond to the exaltation of Christ?
6. Would someone share a personal experience in which he or she exercised a selfless attitude? What were the results?
7. What words does Paul use to describe Christ's selfless attitude?
8. What are some things that Christians today are tempted to hold onto selfishly?
9. Who in your life has been a good model of selflessness?
10. What did God do in response to Christ's selfless sacrifice?
11. Of what do you need to "empty" yourself in order to adopt a selfless attitude?
12. How can Christians today display a selfless attitude?

—*From Montavilla Baptist Church's* Caringroup Leadership Training Workbook *(1980); Portland, Oregon*

6
Formulating Good Questions

Forming good discussion questions is one of the most demanding endeavors for the small-group leader. But there are criteria by which we can evaluate our questions to determine their purpose, form, and ability to provoke thought and discussion.

Remember the aim of questions: It is not to lecture or share what you have learned from your study but to lead the group into discovering for themselves what the passage teaches.

■ A good question is a key that unlocks the meaning.
■ A good question is a tool to dig into the passage.

■ Three basic types of questions are:

1. Observation—fact. What does it say?
2. Interpretation—meaning. What does it mean?
3. Application—to my life. What does it mean to me?

The Question of Observation

These types of questions start with such words as *who, what, describe, find, list*. Make sure the facts are discovered before launching into an interpretation. When Bible studies go off on tangents, often it is at this point. We start interpreting before we have the facts. It may take several observation questions to get all the facts.

The questions here have to be simple, but not so simple that they insult the intelligence. Sometimes it helps to combine two questions. Example: "When did Nicodemus come to see Jesus and why do you suppose he came then?" It helps (particularly at the beginning of the group) to explain the purpose of the fact questions: namely, to get the facts out in the open before interpreting them.

The Question of Interpretation

These questions may start with such phrases as *what does it mean, why, how*, and *explain*. Keep the group to the text. We are not bringing our ideas to the Scripture; we are letting the Scripture speak to us.

The Question of Application

"What does it mean to me here and now?" "What must I do?" Questions of application are often neglected. They are hardest to formulate, but they are the link between Bible study and daily living. You have to live with the passage, asking God to help you see where it applies.

■ ■ ■

These three types of questions are tools. Many questions of fact will lead to one good application. Questions will go from simple (fact) to more complex (interpretation and application). Little time should be spent on questions of fact in comparison with much time on application.

Here are some tests to apply to your questions. Never ask a question that can be answered with "yes" or "no." It does not promote discussion.

■ Is it brief and clear?
■ Does it have a definite answer from the passage or does it lead to speculation?
■ Does it stimulate thought?

■ Does it make a point worth considering at this time?
■ Do the questions proceed logically and build one on the other?

—*Adapted from* Building Christian Community Through Small Groups, *a syllabus by* Roberta Hestenes

7
Beyond Bible Study Questions

Every small group needs an occasional zap—not by lightning, but by a healthy dose of creativity from you, the leader. There are other ways to learn from a Bible study than by systematically reciting answers to questions one through nine. For example:

■ Use *visuals.* Bring a bridle when you study James 3, or a poster of the human body when you study 1 Corinthians 12. Bring in a map when you study Paul's missionary journeys and calculate the distance he traveled in terms familiar to you, i.e., from Chicago to Indianapolis.
■ Use *drama.* If it's not your gift, enlist a group member or two to prepare a short skit to illustrate the lesson. Or initiate role play of a situation that applies to your study.
■ Occasionally use *taped messages* by pastors and teachers that will enhance what you've already studied on your own. Or is there a scene from a *video* that demonstrates a biblical principle such as forgiveness or redemption? Show that scene as a prelude to your discussion.
■ Clip *cartoons.* Keep a file's worth, and use them to illustrate the same human foibles that your Bible study addresses.
■ *Contemporize* your study. Instead of picturing Jesus turning water into wine back in Cana, get your group to imagine Him creating more chicken wings when the finger food at your wedding reception runs low. What kind of reactions might you expect from the guests? How would the local newspaper report such an event?
■ *Regress to childhood.* What are ways your teachers held you in thrall when you were younger? Puppets, chalk talks, slides, music, or hands-on activities like clay modeling or drawing

work with adults as well as with children. And we all need a little more play in our stress-filled lives.

Your church or public libraries are good sources for books on creative teaching methods. The best teaching tools will capture people's attention, arouse curiosity, stimulate discussion, and clarify abstract concepts in concrete ways. They'll also turn your small-group meetings from mundane to memorable.

—*Sue Kline, Colorado Springs, Colorado*

8
The Ten C's of Quality Questions

■ *Concise*. Good questions cover only one idea at a time.

■ *Complete*. Make sure participants have all the information they need to answer a question.

■ *Clear*. Keep it understandable. Be sure questions are not over the heads of group members.

■ *Connected*. Don't ask a question that will lead your group on a tangent.

■ *Conversational*. The aim is not just to ask questions and have the group answer them; it is to facilitate conversation among everyone.

■ *Contestable*. The best discussion questions do not have one right answer. They are open-ended, which forces people to think.

■ *Challenging*. Ask questions that make people stretch their minds. Silence after a question may mean people are really thinking about their answers.

■ *Creative*. Get group members to look at an issue from a side they may not have thought of before. For example, tell a story containing an unresolved issue and ask participants to solve it. The only bad question is the one you use all the time.

■ *Controversial*. Make a controversial statement and see how the group responds. Just remember to use this method sparingly and with discernment.

■ *Considerate*. Do not embarrass or get too personal too soon. Particularly in new groups, questions that dig too deep may keep people from coming back next week.

What's Questionable About These Questions?
From the ten principles in the preceding list, what makes each of these a bad question?

1. Give three reasons Jesus asked the apostles who they thought He was, and tell me how you would answer His question.
2. What are the theological implications of Peter's acclamation with regard to Trinitarian versus Unitarian doctrines, and what does that imply about the ontological argument?
3. What three attitudes was Jesus looking for when He asked this question?
4. What is one area in which you do not make Jesus the Lord of your life? How does that make you feel?
5. What was going through the Apostle John's mind as Peter answered Jesus' question?

Answers
1. Asks more than one question. Sounds like it's looking for a specific answer.
2. Over the heads of all but the Bible-college professors in your group. Asks more than one question. Could embarrass your group members.
3. This isn't a discussion question; it's a test. Looks for one "correct" answer (actually three). Is not complete—how would anyone know what attitudes Jesus was looking for?
4. Asks more than one question. Is inconsiderate of those who might not be willing to be this transparent.
5. The only logical answer is, "How should I know?" Is incomplete. Could be improved (and made more challenging) by asking, "If you were the Apostle John, what would have been going through your mind . . . ?"

—*Michael Mack, Cincinnati, Ohio*

9
The Art of Feedback

Feedback is a way of helping another person to consider changing his behavior. It is communication to a person (or group) that gives that person information about how he or she affects others. As in a guided missile system, feedback helps an individual keep his behavior on target and thus more effectively achieve his goals.

Some criteria for useful feedback:

■ *It is descriptive rather than evaluative:* By describing one's own reaction, it leaves another individual free to use it or not as he sees fit. Avoiding evaluative language reduces the tendency of the other individual to react defensively.

■ *It is specific rather than general:* Telling someone that he is dominating is probably not as useful as saying, "Just now when we were deciding this issue you did not listen to what others said, and I felt forced to accept your arguments or face attack from you."

■ *It takes into account the needs of both the receiver and the giver of feedback:* Feedback can be destructive when it serves only our own needs and fails to consider the needs of the person on the receiving end.

■ *It is directed toward behavior that the receiver can do something about:* Frustration is only increased when a person is reminded of some shortcoming over which he has no control.

■ *It is solicited, rather than imposed:* Feedback is most useful when the receiver himself has formulated and introduced a question for those observing him to answer.

■ *It is well timed:* In general, feedback is most useful at the earliest opportunity after the given behavior occurs (depending, of course, on the person's readiness to hear it, support available from others, etc.).

■ *It is checked to ensure clear communication:* One way of doing this is to have the receiver try to paraphrase the feedback to see if it corresponds to what the sender had in mind.

When feedback is given in a group, both the giver and receiver have the opportunity to check the accuracy of the feedback with others in the group. Is this impression one person's only or is it shared by others?

Feedback is a way of giving help. It is a corrective mechanism for the individual who wants to learn how well his behavior matches his intentions. It is a means to help establish one's identity—one way of answering "Who am I?"
—*Source unknown*

10
Listening and Leading

This activity is designed to sensitize small-group leaders to the importance of listening. It is also an excellent exercise for group members.

1. Prepare in advance a set of cards, one card for each person in the group. Write one of the following instructions on each card:

   ■ When responding to questions, jump to conclusions.
   ■ Interrupt other people when they are talking.
   ■ Start side conversations during group discussion.
   ■ Always disagree with other people's comments.

2. Distribute a card to each group member. (It's okay if two or three people get the same instruction.) Tell them not to reveal what their card says but to follow the instructions during the discussion.

3. Read aloud the following passage: "A woman should learn in quietness and full submission. I do not permit a woman to teach or to have authority over a man; she must be silent. For Adam was formed first, then Eve" (1 Timothy 2:11-13). Lead the group in a brief discussion. The following questions should get you started:

   ■ According to this passage, in what situations should a woman not speak?
   ■ Was Paul setting forth a principle the church should follow today?
   ■ What implications does this passage have for marriages?
   ■ Why does Paul base his argument on Adam and Eve?

4. After five to ten minutes of discussion (or at least long enough for people to get into their roles), call time out. Lead the group to analyze what happened in the discussion—not the opinions presented but the interaction that took place. Ask these questions:

■ How did you feel about following the instructions on your card?
■ What kept the discussion from being productive?
■ How can we be better listeners in this group?

If you're doing this exercise with group leaders, you should also consider the following:

■ Why are group leaders so uncomfortable with . . . ?
■ How does listening help others learn?
■ How can you teach listening skills to a group?

—Clark Cothern, a pastor in Adrian, Michigan

11
Are You Teacher A or Teacher B?

TEACHER A

A Question Asker
By asking questions, this teacher encourages students to think, answer their own questions, make their own discoveries, and take more home from the lesson.

A Group Guide
This teacher guides the group through the lesson in a way that lets them see the scenery for themselves and enjoy the trip personally. Teacher A's students are active, alert, and frequently make personal applications at the end of class. Teacher A finds that he or she learns from the lessons just like the students do.

A Dialogue Traffic Cop
Teacher A points students in the right direction without actually driving them there. Students learn to go to the Bible for answers. They form personal convictions from what they learn.

TEACHER B

An Answer Giver
On the rare occasions when Teacher B asks a question, he rushes to answer it himself. Pauses make him uncomfortable, so he finds it awkward to wait for a student to come up with an answer. Students in this teacher's class tend to be passive.

A Know-It-All Narrator
Sometimes Teacher B's style resembles someone showing slides and telling all about a trip. Teacher B gives all the information and does all the describing. Students tend to drift off and appear inattentive and restless. Rarely does Teacher B hear about a student's personal application.

A Doctrine Cop
Students sometimes make wild statements and express off-the-wall opinions. Teacher B is quick to correct all mistakes and disagree with any opinion that is not like his. He wonders why his students can't seem to find answers in their Bibles—they always wait for him to tell them what to believe. They just won't think for themselves!

In the previous chart, Teacher A and Teacher B represent different teaching styles. As you read, underline the phrases that describe the way you teach now. If you find ways you'd like to improve your teaching, circle those phrases. Then begin with your next lesson to incorporate those improvements.

—*Clark Cothern, Adrian, Michigan*

12
Climate Control

No greater love hath anyone than to give up their comfortable chair to a newcomer.

Editor's note: The following activity is designed to teach leaders of small groups how to set the thermostat of a group on "friendly." It can easily be adapted for use in a small group by focusing the questions in step 3 on group members instead of group leaders.

On separate cards, write or type the following climate qualities (one phrase per card):

■ Atmosphere of Anticipation
■ Climate of Care
■ Temperature of Trust
■ Spirit of Serving

1. If there are more than four people present, divide into four teams. Distribute one card to each team.
2. Explain that each team has a different "climate quality" or characteristic of a small group. Ask the members to make two short lists, one on the left side of the card and one on the right.

   ■ The short list on the left will be things that turn down the temperature for that climate quality—actions that pour cold water on the climate quality listed.
   ■ The short list on the right will be things that turn up the temperature for that climate quality—actions that add warmth and a breath of fresh air described by the climate quality listed.

Give them five minutes to make the lists.

3. Regroup after the teams have finished. Ask someone to write down the teams' ideas. One person from each team reads the climate quality (printed on the top of the card) and the two best items on the right side of the card. When everyone has finished, there should be at least eight positive actions a group can take to create a friendly climate.

Discussion questions: What are the possible results of the actions you just listed? How can you involve your group in learning these climate qualities? Could you use this activity to raise the awareness level of your group's climate?

4. Pray for Christlike climate control in your groups.

—Clark Cothern, Adrian, Michigan

13
How to Fail at Small Groups

My church had grown in the past, but we had reached a plateau of around 200 members. People were complaining that they didn't know others seated around them. At a church growth seminar I attended, the leader said the solution was to begin a series of small fellowship groups of eight to twelve people. I knew that was the answer to the growth problem and the cry for intimate fellowship.

I proceeded to form a few small groups. I talked to each group, gave them some material, and encouraged them to enjoy this wondrous, new experience. I don't suppose it will surprise experienced leaders that these groups died within three months.

I quickly realized that while many books and lecturers proclaim that the small group should be the basic structure of the church, few point out the problems to avoid. From my experience, I've identified five pitfalls that can lead to the demise of a small group.

One: LACK OF LEADER TRAINING OR GUIDANCE
The leader is the most important element in a group. My initial mistake was to assume that leadership could be transferred from person to person with equal success. I learned the hard way that people should have some experience in small groups before they try to lead.

The best way to train leaders is to form a model group. Choose those you believe would make good leaders and model what will be expected of them. As they see you leading discussions, sharing, and dealing with conflict in the group, they will begin to understand what it takes to be a leader.

Two: LACK OF AN UNDERSTOOD CONTRACT
From the beginning, members should know the group's purpose and what is expected of them. If people understand that the group will last for eight weeks and has a twofold purpose of Bible study and fellowship, chances are good that they will attend faithfully and achieve those purposes.

This lack has killed more than one group I've started. One man in an early group complained, "I came here to study the Bible, not to spill my guts to the people here." I had never told him that one of my purposes for forming the group was to build relationships among the members. He came expecting to spend the whole time in study and felt betrayed when we didn't.

Three: NOT TAKING TIME FOR RELATIONSHIPS
The covenant of a small group should clearly state that part of your purpose is to grow in fellowship with each other. New Testament writers tell us fifty-eight times to be engaged in specific activities in relationship with other people, which will enable us to serve more effectively and grow spiritually. What better place to perform these responsibilities than a small group?

People have an inborn need to know and be known. One of the best ways to facilitate relationships in a small group is to use questions that encourage people to say something about themselves, such as, "Where did you go on your first date with your spouse, and how did you feel that night? What is your favorite place in your home, and why? When did God become more than a word to you?"

Four: CHOOSING LECTURE OVER DISCUSSION
People don't remember much of a lecture. They learn much better if there is a discussion in which they can discover truth for themselves. Remember these two guidelines: Don't ask questions that have a correct answer (such as, "Is Jesus Christ really God?"), and let the group members be the experts. Ask them a question they will know something about, and let them discuss it.

Five: NOT KNOWING WHEN TO END
Groups pass through a series of stages: (a) precontract, when they discuss their purposes and goals; (b) orientation, when they get used to each other; (c) power and control, a time in which people decide who is in

control and what roles they will take; (d) trust, when they enjoy the group and each other—it usually takes several meetings to get to this point; (e) differentiation, where people begin to lose interest because they are ready for a change; and (f) conclusion or new beginning, a time to celebrate what the group has meant to them and move on or begin again.

When you see differentiation taking place, don't try to pump life into a dying group. Celebrate what the group has meant to you and move on. If you end the group on a positive note, rather than allowing it to die slowly, the members will be more likely to move on to other groups.

People in small groups often experience explosive spiritual growth. Such groups are vitally needed today. But approach them with careful planning, because it is much harder to start again after people have experienced failure. As you build, avoiding the pitfalls, may your experiences prove positive!

—*Bruce T. Ballast, Chino, California*

14
Six Steps to a Successful Brainstorm

Need to plan a weekend retreat? In search of fresh ideas for outreach projects? Facing a seemingly unsolvable problem in your small group? Consider a brainstorming session. One good idea leads to another, then another, and people are energized as they discover different ways of doing things.

For a successful brainstorm, follow these steps.

- *Promote* **the evening** as a time of fun, energy, and mental stimulation, not just another meeting.
- *Create* **the right environment.** Use balloons, streamers, and confetti to brighten the room. Bring toys: a large stuffed animal, a yo-yo, bottles of Wonder Bubble with wands. Spread brightly wrapped candy around the table. Have energizing music playing as group members arrive.
- *Know* **what you want to accomplish**. If your purpose is only to generate ideas that will be sifted through later, then fifteen minutes per topic may be sufficient. If your plan is to generate ideas plus sift and refine, allow more time.

■ *Plan* **ahead.** If you plan to facilitate the meeting, select someone in advance to write down the ideas. Obtain a white board, flip chart, or huge sheets of newsprint plus colorful markers so ideas can be written large enough for all to see. Formulate questions that will prompt creative thinking.

■ *Communicate* **the ground rules** for effective brainstorming: Every idea is accepted and written down (even the outrageous and silly ones). No idea is evaluated during the brainstorming stage. No negative comments are allowed ("We tried that last year and it didn't work").

■ *Stick* **to your time limit.** Don't wear your group out by letting the brainstorming go on too long.

Energy, enthusiasm, a sense of adventure, and a positive attitude are the keys to a successful brainstorm. If people are having fun, they'll generate their best ideas.

—Jean Slagel, Beaverton, Oregon

15
Spiritual Authority— Use It, Don't Abuse It

Do you desire to be an effective influence in the lives of other people? If so, you should be aware of the essentials of spiritual authority. Ignorance of them is the major reason why inexperienced small-group leaders often feel inadequate, and violation of them is a primary source of abuse by leaders who—usually unwittingly—misuse power in a group.

For the Christian, the ultimate model of spiritual authority is Jesus Christ. Jesus' authority comes from God (John 13:3). The Father chose Him for the work of man's redemption. In the same way, Jesus has chosen us to be a "royal priesthood"—to go out among men and women of the world and urge them toward Christ's Kingdom.

Every Christian has spiritual authority (1 Corinthians 2:15), and God chooses some Christians for leadership positions. There is inherent authority in the office of a leader (e.g., David always respected the mad Saul as "the Lord's anointed"—1 Samuel 24:6). But we can increase the effectiveness of our exercise of authority by observing the following guidelines:

1. Servanthood is the crucial prerequisite to spiritual authority.
Jesus did not "grasp" His authority as a privilege of position, but gave up its rights and took on "the very nature of a servant" (Philippians 2:7). Jesus' act becomes authoritative for the Christian: We, too, are to become "as nothing," and in humility treat others as better than ourselves.

Self-denial is bitter medicine in an age that has made "self-esteem" a priority. But the only way to exercise authority in the spiritual realm is to die to self so that God may raise us in His power and for His purposes. Only by taking on the very nature of a servant can we be agents of God's authority and bear fruit that will last for eternity.

2. The Bible is the greatest resource for spiritual authority. The Scriptures record that all Israel recognized the spiritual authority of the prophet Samuel—even when Samuel was a youth. "The Lord was with Samuel as he grew up, and he let none of his words fall to the ground . . . and Samuel's word came to all Israel" (1 Samuel 3:19, 4:1). What was Samuel's secret of spiritual authority? "The Lord . . . revealed himself to Samuel through his word" (3:21). If we desire to influence others with genuine spiritual authority, we must be not only servants of men, but also "servants of the word" (Luke 1:2).

3. Praying for wisdom is a necessity for spiritual authority. Young King Solomon prayed to God, "I am only a little child and do not know how to carry out my duties . . . so give your servant a discerning heart" (1 Kings 3:7-9). God gave Solomon a discerning heart, and the Scriptures say that all Israel "saw that he had wisdom from God" (3:28).

No matter how inadequate we may feel some days, we can confidently ask God for authoritative wisdom, because He has promised it to us (James 1:5).

4. Spiritual authority is always informed by the needs, the hurts, and the burdens of others. Jesus was sensitive to people. He recognized the truth about them (e.g., the woman at the well), and He loved them in their human frailty (e.g., the rich young ruler).

This kind of authority never seeks self-fulfillment, nor does it try to impress others. Rather, it is genuine and sincere, focusing on God and other people. The person with spiritual authority is neither self-demeaning nor self-inflating; he is self-forgetful in his loving attention to others. He is an encourager; he urges others toward a deeper knowledge of God and a more excellent contribution to His Kingdom.

5. Spiritual authority carries out the work of God with firm conviction. At one point, members of David's army talked of stoning him. But he mobilized their loyalty by seeking God and acquiring a firm sense of purpose toward God's ends (1 Samuel 30:3-10). We see this resolute strength in Jesus as He walked toward Golgotha, carrying the cross.

Our lives will acquire spiritual authority when they are consumed by the glorious Person of God, and when we do the works He has prepared for us (Ephesians 2:10) with serene but definite care.

—*Don Simpson, Director of Communications, The Navigators, Colorado Springs, Colorado*

16
Ouch! That Hurts!

We all dread the moment. But, as leaders, we know it will come. One of our group members bears down on us, her face red, her brow furrowed in frustration. Before we can think of anything to say, the complaints start spewing out.

Even if people are well-intentioned, their criticism hurts. How can we respond in a Christlike manner?

1. *Do* keep a cool head. Anger will cloud your reasoning.
2. *Do* say a quick prayer, asking God to keep you from defensiveness and to show you the truth in the person's words.
3. *Do* hear the criticism without allowing it to affect your self-worth. God can use criticism to point out flaws He hopes to change.
4. *Do* hear the message behind the complaint. Sometimes criticism is the way people say, "I need help. I feel bad. I want you to fix it."
5. *Do* be ready to admit any fault of your own, no matter how small.
6. *Do* ask the person to be part of the solution. Perhaps he can fill in where he thinks you're falling short.
7. *Do* thank the person for her concern (whether her words show concern or not).
8. *Don't* immediately jump to your own defense. In time, you may need to present your side of the story, but to do so initially will only make your critic try harder to convince you of your fault.
9. In fact, *don't* answer at all, immediately, especially if you find your emotions starting to flare. Instead, ask for time to think and pray about what was said. Tell your critic you'll get back to him later (then be sure to do so).

10. *Don't* worry about being right. Differences need to be honestly and appropriately confronted, but they won't always be resolved.

Finally, remember that Jesus, too, was criticized and condemned. But, "when they hurled their insults at him, he did not retaliate; when he suffered, he made no threats. Instead he entrusted himself to him who judges justly" (1 Peter 2:23). Criticism and even injustice are an opportunity to reflect the character of Christ.

—*Marlo M. Schalesky, Gilroy, California*

17
Outward Bound

If your group is experiencing staleness, take a look at your focus. While engaging Bible study is a prerequisite to true Christian community, an exclusively inward focus can stunt the growth of most any group. The inward journey was made to turn outward. Such a turn usually begins with the leader. What can a small-group leader do to encourage an outward focus?

■ *Get burdened.* My fire is stoked by reading of others who burned brightly for Christ. Two of my favorites are David Brainerd and George Whitefield. Biographies, journals, and diaries of godly men and women are excellent vision-builders.

■ *Develop redemptive friendships.* Help your neighbor build his fence. Become a reader at a local convalescent hospital. Challenge the junior high kid across the street to a game of HORSE.

■ *Model involvement.* When you do any of the above, take a group member with you. Don't treat it like class time. Just let him see how easy it is to "hang out" with others for Christ's sake.

■ *Regularly highlight outreach as a group fundamental.* Ask for outreach testimonies as often as you ask for prayer requests. Emphasize a specific opportunity at each meeting. By giving outreach more than periodic airtime, a leader can counteract the false belief that outreach is optional.

■ *Facilitate a group activity.* Get a list of newcomers who have visited your church and invite a family or individual to one of your small-group outings. Or fill a number of grocery bags for a family in need. Adopt a pregnant teen through your local pregnancy center. Repair the roof of a widow's home. Sponsor, coach, and cheer on a local Little League team. Work a booth at a community festival. Join a community softball team. Just do it together.

■ *Celebrate your group achievements.* Periodically throw a party to praise God and reward group members for jobs well done. Remember, Jesus celebrated with the disciples upon the return of the seventy (Luke 10:17-24).

—Barry McGee, Palo Cedro, California

18
Developing Your Members' Ministry Muscles

As a servant leader of a small group you are called to do more than prepare for meetings and maintain a close relationship with the Lord. You are called to "consider others better than yourself" (Philippians 2:3). You can do this in your group by allowing each member to carry some of the weight of leadership and so develop his or her personal ministry skills (Ephesians 4:11-13). Here are some ways I've found to do that:

1. *Give everyone the opportunity to lead group worship activities.* Most people are willing to suggest songs they'd like to sing or read prayers if they have some time to select or write them. Ask for volunteers a week ahead of time. If someone feels uncomfortable at the start, offer to help lead the song(s) he or she has chosen. If your group doesn't know a particular song, it is always fun to have a group member teach it to you.

2. *Depend on group members to pray in the meetings, even if they seem hesitant.* Most of your own praying should be done ahead of time.

3. *Let group members work out conflicts and make decisions by themselves.* You may want to start them out by outlining problems and proposing options to solve them, but let them make decisions by prayer and consensus. Indicate your openness for input, feedback, and criticism as well.

4. ***Encourage the ministry of hospitality,*** if you are meeting in homes, by giving different people each week the opportunity to host a meeting or to provide refreshments.

5. ***Don't talk too much.*** You can do most of your teaching with good discussion questions. Formulate a number of questions that will lead the group to discover insights for themselves. They will invariably teach you in return!

6. ***Teach some group members how to study and prepare to lead the meetings.*** Those who are called to teach will want to learn. Encourage them to lead a session or two to begin with. This is less intimidating than being responsible for a whole series. Offer your prayer support and availability to help in preparation — otherwise, back off.

7. ***Pray regularly,*** not only for the meetings but also for the group members and their individual ministries. If at first you don't know individual members well enough to pray specifically, try some of the prayers that Paul used for the people he ministered to (Ephesians 1:15-19, 3:14-19; Philippians 1:9-11; Colossians 1:9-12; 2 Thessalonians 1:11).

Serving your group by encouraging their gifts and ministries is rewarding — you may even work yourself out of a job!

—Hannelore Bozeman, leader of women's Bible study groups, Iowa City, Iowa

19
Training Others to Lead

Throughout the world today many committed Christians are witnessing the dynamic impact of small groups. The intense fellowship, personal interaction around Scriptures, and commitment to applying Scripture is often unparalleled by other methods of spiritual development. As the members of your group grow spiritually, some may develop the ability and desire to become discussion group leaders. Be sensitive to this, and consider whether you would like to train someone in the group as your assistant. This person could eventually replace you or be the leader of another group.

When choosing an assistant, look for someone who will . . .

■ *pray with you regularly* for the other group members.

■ *help you evaluate each session after it is over.* You can discuss what happened and why, and how to improve. Your assistant may be able to see what is happening more clearly than you because he or she is not under the pressure of asking questions to keep group discussion going.

■ *learn how to lead the group if you need to be absent.*

■ *be willing to begin and lead another group.* If your group grows too large and you need to divide, your assistant will be the logical person to lead the new group.

If your group does divide, remind them that growing too large would hinder the advantages of small-group discussion—intimate fellowship, personal involvement with everyone, plenty of opportunities for everyone to talk, the ease with which the entire group can meet in anyone's living room, and so on.

The process of multiplication and growth will continue as your former assistant finds someone in the new group to become an assistant to be trained for starting yet another group.

—*Adapted from* How to Lead Small Group Bible Studies *(NavPress, 1982), out of print*

20
Why Split the Group?

Every group has a life span; the trick is to find out where a group is in that span. It is the misfortune of many groups that they do not recognize the time to divide until well after they should. Cell-like division in groups can produce new life by including new members and revitalizing old ones.

Telltale Signs

Groups exhibit telltale signs as they near the end of their life span. If your group is experiencing some or all of these signs, it might be time to divide.

When a cell group has been together for too long, *it can become ingrown.* It views newcomers as intruders, and it expresses no desire to nurture or enfold the new members. Group members feel threatened by new members, make little effort to get to know them, and tend to engage in conversations the new people know nothing about.

The *quality of fellowship also suffers* when a group nears the end of its life span. Many members will settle into the comfort of "sameness," no longer struggling with the issues of faith they did in the earlier stages. Instead of prayerfully searching together for new ways to serve God's Kingdom and people, the group members see the group only as a place to focus on "my" needs — "a time to let my hair down."

When a group has outlived its life cycle, *laziness may set in.* The group may spend more and more time talking about the football team's season record, and less and less time on serious Bible study. The leader may quit exploring new ideas and preparing good questions, and depend on existing group relationships to carry discussion.

Principles for Division

1. Take steps to reorganize your group before life span pitfalls become entrenched. Don't let the group dwindle to a number that can't provide sufficient interaction. If your group is still somewhat hesitant to divide, it means that their enthusiasm is high. This kind of enthusiasm will help fuel a successful second group.

2. Emphasize that division is a growth step. Don't announce that you are dividing the group (no one will want to do that). Stress that you are forming a second discussion meeting. Enthusiastic members want to be a part of growth, but not of division.

3. Try to head off excessive defensiveness about "our tried and true group." Some groups do have something very special together and should not be divided — as long as they have not exhibited the telltale signs of life span stagnation. But consider the idea that if quality fellowship has occurred in one group, it should be transplanted into others.

New groups will benefit from people who have known the dynamics of successful group fellowship. What better place to find these people than in your own "tried and true group"?

—*Jim Walker, Navigator contact staff member and small-group leader,
San Jose, California*

21
Dividing Your Group

One difficulty that, oddly enough, can happen because of success in a small group, is growth. A group cannot remain at optimum effectiveness when it grows beyond a certain number.

The chart below suggests how to evaluate healthy size. The formula R=N (N-1) determines the number of relationships (R) in the group, based upon the number of people in the group (N).

Size of Group (N)	No. of Relationships (R)	
4	(4 x 3)	12
6	(6 x 5)	30
8	(8 x 7)	56
10	(10 x 9)	90
12	(12 x 11)	132
15	(15 x 14)	210
20	(20 x 19)	380
40	(40 x 39)	1,560

The larger the group, the less the possibility for interpersonal relationships and opportunity for give and take. Most of us can deal with 120 relationship possibilities, so twelve is generally agreed to be the upper limit.

Specific Suggestions If Your Group Decides to Divide
  1. Don't try to spin a new group off with a leader from outside the original group. People gravitate toward the familiar, so choose someone from among current membership to lead one of the new groups. Make sure you always have a member in your group who is a "leader in training," in case your group should divide.
  2. Continually emphasize the reason for the division. Reflect on the situation as a good problem, with new opportunities for each member to become more like Jesus Christ.
  3. Leaders should make every effort to stay in close contact. They can support one another and keep the groups going in the same direction.
  4. Have reunions. Plan times when the entire original group gets together for social occasions or projects. This eases the pain of separation and allows the members to catch up with one another.
—Chart is from Key to Parish Life, *a manual by Rev. Robert D. Nix, Jr., Saint Stephen's Church, Sewickley, Pennsylvania*

PART TWO

SMALL-GROUP IDEAS

Hands-On Ideas for Immediate Use in Small Groups

Bible Study

22
Sharpening One Another in Bible Study

Here's a Bible study format in which the members choose their own questions. In other words, they sharpen one another "as iron sharpens iron" (Proverbs 27:17) by choosing the issues from each passage they'll focus on. The approach encourages everyone to participate!

One: Choose what the group will study. It's best to choose either a book of the Bible or a book with a biblical theme.

Two: Assign a chapter a week. Tell each member to choose one or two questions from the reading assignment that he or she will want to discuss at the next meeting. The questions can be either hard-to-understand passages or ideas that seem particularly helpful or challenging.

Three: At the following meeting give each member two minutes (and insist on two, or you'll run out of time) to share his or her two questions or insights.

Four: Choose a "scribe" at the beginning of each meeting. This person records each member's questions or insights.

Five: When all members have shared their questions, the scribe will read them back to the group and the group will decide together which questions or insights they'd like to cover during the course of the meeting. Be sure to set a time limit for deciding and be reasonable about how much you can actually cover in your time together.

Six: The scribe should start the group off with the first question. Usually everyone will join in the discussion immediately. The preliminary exercise of choosing the topics has warmed everyone up, and the members feel some ownership of and identity with the discussion topics, having chosen them themselves.

One more idea: An alternative to a Scripture or book discussion might be a night at the movies, the theater, or a morality play, of which your members are "the critics." Meet for discussion afterward, using the format above.

—Norma Steven, Bible study leader and conference speaker, Santa Ana, California

23
Questions to Ask Before You Choose a Bible Study Guide

With hundreds of Bible study resources on the market, selecting a study can be a daunting task. Answer these questions to determine if a study guide is right for your group:

■ Is this study biblically based? Is it consistent with the teachings of my church? Will the study lead us into better understanding of what Scripture says, or are we likely to be "sharing our ignorance"?

■ Will this study build good Bible study habits that will make us better students of God's word?

■ Is the depth appropriate for our group?

■ Am I willing and able to commit the preparation time required to lead this study? How much advance preparation is required from group members, and is it realistic?

■ Is the subject engaging? Is it relevant to our lives?

■ Can the chapters be completed in a reasonable amount of time so that we can still pray and mingle?

■ How many lessons are there? What is the group's attention span—will we grow tired of the study before we complete it? What kind of cycle are we on—will we complete the study before our summer break?

■ Will I be encouraged to apply what I learn to personal growth and ministry?

Arrive at a group consensus before choosing a study guide. Seek a study that leaves you with a sense of anticipation for the wonderful things God will teach your group as you gather around His Word.
—*Keith D. Wright, Kansas City, Missouri*

24
Bible Study Variations

Who's Who?

Here's a game that helps acquaint your group members with Bible characters. It requires some research and preparation. Have each person write four or five clues clues describing a person from the Bible. The clues should start out difficult and become easier. For example, the first clue might be, "God said, 'He is a chosen instrument of mine to carry my name before the Gentiles.'" The second clue could read, "He held the clothes of a martyr." The next clue: "He was once blind for three days." Sometimes three or four clues will be needed; at other times, one clue may suffice. Consider doing a "who's who" each week, until every group member has had a chance to try to stump the others. Make available to your group a good study Bible or Bible dictionary so they can select obscure characters as well as familiar ones.

—*Sue Payton de Barajas, Bogota, Colombia*

Nine to Five

As an opener for a Bible study on riches from 1 Timothy 6:6-10, I asked group members to tell about their first jobs and how much they were paid. The results were very interesting. (How would you like to break eggs into a stainless steel vat for eight hours?) This icebreaker taught us new things about each other while leading naturally into our Bible study for the evening.

—*Grant Sikstrom, Red Deer, Alberta, Canada*

25
Put on Your Application SPECS

Biblical teaching should have as its goal not merely imparting information, but imparting information that leads to changed lives. The teacher who wants to change lives builds a collection of effective methods for leading students to practical application.

In *How to Be the Best Sunday School Teacher You Can Be,* Terry Hall suggests this simple acrostic to help teenage and adult group members to discern action steps from a passage of Scripture.

■ Sins (attitudes or actions to forsake)
■ Promises (assurance or benefits from God to claim)
■ Examples (good attitudes or actions to imitate)
■ Commands (directions from God)
■ Stumbling blocks (things God warns us to avoid)

Have your students write SPECS down the left side of an index card. Explain to them what each letter stands for, then give them five minutes to re-read the passage just studied and list a verse or phrase by each applicable category. (Not every category will apply to every passage you teach.)

For example, from Philippians 4:4-9, a student might select verse 4 as a command to obey (Always rejoice) or verse 6 (Don't be anxious) as a stumbling block to avoid. From a variety of possible applications, each group member should then select one specific action to put into practice and write at the bottom of the card how he or she plans to follow through.

—*Sue Kline, Colorado Springs, Colorado*

26
Launching an Investigative Bible Study

When my wife and I wanted to start a Bible study with unbelievers in our building, I went to our pastor for advice.

"Build friendships with the people there first, pray for them, then invite some of them to a Bible study when the time seems right," he said.

"How will we know when the time is right?" I asked.

"Somehow the Holy Spirit will let you know that," our pastor assured me.

I would have preferred a specific date and time and a list of how to's. But we did what he suggested and watched for signs that the time was right.

About eighteen months later, I learned that Sigma had been approached by a cult member and invited to study the Bible. While I was talking with Sigma one day about this cult, a young guy in an AC-DC T-shirt, who reputedly smoked pot, said, "Why don't we start our own Bible study? Mike could lead it, and we could meet at different apartments each week. We could invite other people from the building, too!"

A week later we started a study that continued all summer. In time, we saw two people accept God's grace and forgiveness. Both are growing in knowledge and obedience.

From this experience we learned two essentials for starting an evangelistic Bible study: Warm relationships and dependence on the Holy Spirit's timing and "behind the scenes" working.

Logistical Considerations
■ Keep the meetings short, usually no longer than an hour. Begin and end on time.
■ Set a definite duration, such as ten weeks. People won't commit to something that seems like it might last forever.
■ Meet in someone else's home. It's better to be on their turf.
■ Encourage participants to invite others.
■ It's okay to have a Christian friend or two come with an unbeliever, but don't let the Christians answer all the questions.
■ Don't get discouraged if only a few people show up sometimes. You're planting seeds. God brings the increase.
■ Most important, keep praying. God changes hearts. Prayer reinforces your total dependence on Him.

Choosing a Study
I prefer to start with the gospels, especially with people who know little about the Bible. Bring them face-to-face with their Savior and let them fall in love with Him! In *Introducing Jesus*, Peter Scazzero suggests these six passages for study: Luke 3:2-18, Mark 4:1-20, Mark 1:15-24, John 4:4-26, Luke 15:11-32, and Mark 10:17-21. Or you could ask participants to read the Gospel of John on their own, then come to the discussion time with their questions.

If people are more familiar with the gospel—perhaps they grew up going to church but never accepted Jesus as Savior—consider passages from the epistles that deal with salvation.

I've found it fruitful to take one meeting to view a movie such as *Jesus* or *Jesus of Nazareth* and discuss it.

Be prepared at some point to clearly present the gospel, either to the entire group or one on one as individuals seem ready. Certain tracts or

books, such as John Hendee's *A Peace Treaty with God* may be helpful.
—*Michael Mack, Cincinnati, Ohio*

27
The Hand Illustration:
How to Grab Hold of the Word

Pick up your Bible. How securely can you grasp it with one finger? Silly question. How firm is your hold with two fingers? A child could still pull it away from you. It isn't until you grab your Bible with your whole hand that you get a firm grip.

The Hand Illustration is an easy-to-remember tool for showing someone how to get a working grasp of the Scriptures. Each finger represents one way to take in the Word of God. A balanced intake of the Bible comes through hearing, reading, studying, and memorizing. Then, as we meditate on the Scriptures during these four activities, they become more personal and specific in helping us grow in Christlikeness.

Let's look in more detail at these five methods of learning from the Bible:

- *Hearing* the Word of God from godly pastors and teachers provides us with insight from Bible study done by others. It also stimulates our own appetite for the Scriptures. The weakest finger represents hearing, because we retain the least through that method of intake.
- *Reading* gives us an overall picture of the Bible and is also the foundation of the daily quiet time.
- *Studying* the Scriptures deepens our convictions. It requires greater time and effort but results in increased Bible knowledge.
- *Memorizing* God's Word enables us to use the Sword of the Spirit to overcome temptations and to have verses readily available for ministering to both Christians and nonChristians. Scripture memory stimulates meaningful meditation. The index finger, our strongest finger, represents memorization. We remember 100 percent of what we memorize if we consistently review it.
- *Meditation* is the inward process that should accompany each of the other four methods of Scripture intake. This is why meditation is assigned to the thumb. Only the thumb can touch all the

other four fingers. By meditating on God's Word as we hear, read, study, and memorize, we discover its transforming power at work in us.

Ask group members to trace one hand on a sheet of paper. Have them write the word *hear* on the little finger. Read Romans 10:17 together. On the next finger, have them write the word *read,* then look up Revelation 1:3. The middle finger should be labeled *study.* Read Acts 17:11 together to see an example of men and women who studied the Word of God with dedication. Label the index finger with the word *memorize,* then read Psalm 119:9-11. Finally, have them write the word *meditate* on the thumb. Look up Psalm 1:2-3 to see the benefits of meditating on the Word.

Discuss how meditation can strengthen each of the other four methods for taking in God's Word. Brainstorm ways to increase your intake of Scripture during the next month.

—Adapted from THE 2:7 SERIES, *Course Four (NavPress, 1979)*

28
What Motivates Us to Follow Christ?

The Navigators have identified six primary biblical motives by which we respond to our Lord.

1. Obedience to Christ—Romans 1:14, 1 Corinthians 9:16-17
2. Love for God and man— Matthew 22:39, 2 Corinthians 5:14
3. The glory of God—Isaiah 42:8, 43:7
4. The fear of the Lord—2 Corinthians 5:11
5. The gospel reveals man's only hope—John 6:68
6. Colabor with God—1 Corinthians 3:9

People usually respond most strongly to two of these motivations. Have each member of your group mark the two that he or she is most motivated by. Then share those with the group.

Study the references together and discuss why each person chose the options he did (you may be surprised to find that most groups will gather a majority around one or two of the options).

A suggestion for study outside the group: Each member can do an in-depth study of the options he did not choose as primary motivations. Lower motivation in a particular area is often a result of a low level of familiarity. We tend to focus on what we know.

Encourage your group members to seek out and strengthen what is less familiar to them by studying the references provided and any others they can find. Set aside another group meeting to share what you've all discovered.

—*Navigator staff*

29
The ABCs of Growing a Strong Group

Our small groups follow a method of study I was given by the late Dawson Trotman, founder of The Navigators. I've used it with everyone from junior high schoolers to adults. It is not difficult, but it does take perseverance. Before the group meeting, each member studies the passage and prepares this outline:

A. Give the chapter *A Title.*
B. Pick out and write down the *Best Verse,* one that reflects the chapter's theme.
C. Find a *Challenge.* Write in your own words a thought from the chapter that meant much to you. Add a few sentences describing how you can personally apply that truth.
D. List any *Difficulties.* Write down anything you are unsure of or cannot understand.
E. This stands for *Essence.* In your own words, write a summary of the verse or passage. Stick to what it says, not what it means. A rule of thumb is to allow five words per verse. This is not binding; it is only a guide so you will not be too brief or too wordy.

When our small groups come together, we share what we have found from the passage under consideration.

—*The Reverend Richard DeLong, Evangelical Community Church, Bloomington, Indiana; this method is also presented in* The Navigator Bible Studies Handbook *(NavPress, 1979, 1994)*

30
Jesus' Questions:
Reflections for Your Group

"He came not to answer questions, but to ask them; not to settle men's souls, but to provoke them." So says Herman Horne in his one-hundred-year-old classic, *Jesus the Master Teacher.* Fortunately, over one hundred of Jesus' questions are recorded in the gospels for us to study, understand, and emulate in our small groups. Here are some reflections on those questions:

Jesus majored in questions that led and guided. He asked questions that suggested the answer He was after yet demanded clear and careful thought. He forced the hearers of His questions to draw the conclusions themselves.

Jesus' questions were what we might call "leading" questions. In its right form, a leading question leads one on—challenging him or her to a specific conclusion that is not a "pat" or careless answer.

Jesus did this in Matthew 5:13 when He said to His disciples, "You are the salt of the earth. But if the salt loses its saltiness, how can it be made salty again?" The answer is fairly simple, but the conclusion demands recognition of a hard truth: You have to stay salty to have the good effect of salt.

Questions made up the heart of Jesus' teaching method and ministry. Look at some of the reasons He asked questions:

■ To secure information (Luke 8:30).
■ To express emotion (John 3:10).
■ To recall information (Mark 2:25-26).
■ To awaken the conscience (Matthew 23:17).
■ To elicit faith (Mark 8:29).
■ To create a dilemma (Mark 3:4).

Sometimes Jesus asked questions to stop opposition. He asked others that His enemies were unwilling to answer. Compare Matthew 21:25-27, 22:45; Luke 14:5-6.

As you study Jesus' questions, notice their distinctive tone. How He asked His questions was as important as why and what He asked.

—*David P. Bertch, group leader for Career Impact Ministries, Fort Worth, Texas*

31
Using a Bible Study Guide

Are you leading a group through a Bible study guide? Here are a few user's tips to help you make the most of your materials.

First, *prepare thoroughly before leading your group through the next lesson.* As you work through the material, anticipate areas of uncertainty or questions that may come up among group members. Prepare for these questions by doing some extra homework before your meeting: either find answers to the questions you anticipate, or locate potential resources you can recommend so group members can look up the answers on their own.

Second, *base your approach for leading the meeting on the nature of the study guide.* Following are three possible approaches to covering study material during your group session. Select or adapt the one most appropriate to the study material your group is using. (Some Bible study guides contain or are accompanied by leader's guides. Be sure to consult such a help if it is available to you.)

Approach one: *Follow the guide closely by simply sharing your individual answers to each question.* Use this approach if you have the benefit of a particularly well-structured and creatively written Bible study. Does the number of questions in the lesson seem about right for the time you'll have together? Is there a good mix of observation, interpretation, and application questions? Sharing interpretations of Scripture passages may uncover some differing opinions and produce lively debate; sharing applications will help your group make the crucial transfer from knowledge to action—and the variety of responses will create an environment of stimulating and relevant interaction.

If you do choose to follow the guide closely, remember to be flexible. Don't confine your discussion to blindly following a rigid, question-by-question format if opportunity arises to pursue a productive tangent. Pray for the Holy Spirit's guidance in staying sensitive to the direction that will be most beneficial to your group. As Lorne Sanny, former president of The Navigators, has advised leaders heading into group meetings, "Go in with a plan, but also with a sincere desire to come up with a better plan."

Approach two: *Follow the guide loosely by sharing the highlights of your individual study preparations.* This approach is helpful if the Bible study you have selected is either too short or too long to discuss question by question. You may also wish to use this structure if it seems that the Bible study questions have not been written creatively enough to spark productive discussion, yet they still allow some room for personal discovery.

Asking group members to share highlights of their individual study also allows you to center discussion only on those aspects of the lesson that have been most significant to your group.

Approach three: *Depart from following the study guide by using selected discussion questions.* If the study guide is primarily composed of simple observation ("fill-in the blank" type) questions, you'll probably want to prepare some stimulating discussion questions. Look for suggested discussion questions in the study, or any questions built into the lessons that might be particularly adaptable as discussion questions.

If you need to make up your own discussion questions, think of ways to stimulate your group's thinking about implications of their Bible study findings and possible applications.

Your Bible study guide can be a launching pad for a rewarding encounter with God's Word. Prepare thoroughly, plan wisely, and pray carefully—and then expect God to do great things when your group comes together!

—Navigator staff

32
Spiritual Gifts and Pepper in Your Teeth

Identifying our spiritual gift can be like identifying a speck of pepper in our teeth. Sometimes it takes someone else to point it out.

In a group where members know one another well, these activities are effective for understanding and identifying one another's gifts.

1. Ask each person to fill in the blank for the person on their left: "You build up other people and glorify God when you. . . ."
2. Study together passages on spiritual gifts, and ask these questions: "What would our group (or church) be like if everyone was just like you? Why does the Body need all the parts to function properly?"
3. Have group members paraphrase 1 Corinthians 13 by substituting their spiritual gift(s) each time the passage refers to a gift.

For example, "If I have the gift of evangelism, but do not have love, I have become a noisy gong."

4. For each gift represented in your group, make two lists. In the first, note how the gift can be abused when not used with love. In the other, note how each spiritual gift becomes a blessing to others when used with love.

—Clark Cothern, Adrian, Michigan

33
Share Learning, Not Ignorance

People learn better when they are actively involved in the process of learning. But how can you encourage them to share their learning without merely sharing ignorance?

The leader can structure a Bible study to encourage clear thinking. Take a study of Acts 5:1-11, for example. The leader can divide the group into two sub-groups. One group might discuss what sin Ananias and Sapphira actually committed. The other group might look at the church's response to their sin.

The leader should clearly articulate how much time the group will have to do this, and precisely what they should accomplish during the time. The assignment for each sub-group is quite specific and requires them to study only the facts. The groups are not encouraged to interpret any facts before they study them. Often, it is when these two steps are done backwards that shared learning deteriorates into shared ignorance.

Bring the two groups back together and have them share their observations. Encourage them to listen carefully—especially to what the other sub-group found. Then ask for ideas about what the passage can teach them as a group and as individuals. This can be a brainstorm session in which each idea is written down. After the list of ideas is complete, the leader or a designated group member can guide the group through an evaluation of each suggestion. This exercise will help the group come to conclusions together about the importance of what they have discovered. The group will often narrow the list down to the most specific interpretations they've found.

Finally, the leader can ask each member to choose one or more items from the list that represent a crucial need for application in his or her own life and then challenge that person to live it out in the next week. Note that the challenge is one that the group itself has developed, yet it focuses on individual needs.

The leader's role is important—but it means nothing without the participation of group members. The leader is there to monitor the discussion so that important concepts are emphasized and inappropriate concepts are corrected.

These simple suggestions can go a long way toward making group time work productively and significantly in members lives. The group does not share ignorance, instead it brings a variety of ideas into a process that ensures real learning and significant application for each member.

—*Dr. Dennis E. Williams, professor and chairman of the Department of Christian Education at the Denver Theological Seminary, Denver, Colorado*

34
A Six-Step Method
of Bible Study

"I wish I could study the Bible because I want to, rather than because I feel guilty if I don't." With that comment Marsha heaved a sigh and looked around the circle. Many nodded their heads. They knew it was important to have a specific place and time for Bible study, but the third ingredient was missing: how to go about it.

The group talked that day about the very real need for a Bible study method that was enjoyable. The plan they came up with, jokingly nick-named "RCDCQP," is a simple, six-step method. It can be completed in as little as one sitting or as many as five, depending on the amount of time you have each day. Each letter stands for one step.

One: RECORD
As an illustration, let's use Isaiah 26:3. "You will keep in perfect peace him whose mind is steadfast, because he trusts in you." This verse is written in the Record section in the example. If you like to compare translations, write down other translations as well.

Two: CIRCLE
Circle the key words in the verse. In Isaiah 26:3, you could circle *keep, perfect, peace, mind, steadfast, trusts.*

Three: DICTIONARY

Use your dictionary to look up all the words you have circled. For example, the dictionary lists several definitions for keep, but the ones that best fit the usage in Isaiah 26:3 are, "to cause to remain in a specified condition; to guard or protect." Write that definition down next to *keep.* Proceed through your circled words until you are finished. Sometimes the dictionary will give a synonym of the word. Look up that definition also and write it down. Record only the definitions that help you understand the meaning of the verse.

Four: CROSS-REFERENCE

Use your concordance to look up the words you circled in Step 2. Pick only the verses that help you understand the study passage better. Write the reference and next to it a phrase telling what the verse says to you. If you have a study Bible, use the cross-reference texts in the margin. As you practice cross-referencing, sometimes a related verse will pop into your head. Record it as well.

Five: QUESTIONS OR COMMENTS

Any time a question or comment comes to mind, write it down. If you have no questions or comments in this section by the end of Step 4, use the following questions to get started: Who? What? When? Where? Why? How?

Six: PARAPHRASE

This step ties all the other steps together. Look over the dictionary definitions and the cross-reference texts again. Now, instead of the word *keep,* for example, use the definition of *keep.* Tie it in with the definition of *perfect* and *peace* and you will be amazed at the meaning coming through a single verse.

For example, Isaiah 26:3 could be stated like this: "You, God, will guard me from disturbing thoughts or emotions and cause me to remain mentally and emotionally whole and healthy if I will keep my feelings, my thoughts, the way I behave, and the way I reason all focused on You. As I do this, I will trust You and feel that I can depend on you."

—Susan Bishop, Deer Trail, Colorado

35
Letting God Speak

Dick and Ann Honig currently lead four small-group Bible studies. In their weekly meetings they stress the importance of having a daily quiet time, especially hearing from God personally through His Word.

They developed the form below as a way to help people do this. They sometimes use it in a group setting. Dick says, "When we all consider a passage of Scripture using this form, invariably God speaks in different ways to group members, according to their particular needs."

God Speaks to You Personally . . .
Through His Word

Passage _____ Date _____

Paraphrase or summarize main thought:

How God spoke to me personally:

My commitment:

Analysis Questions
■ What is the main idea of the passage?
■ What does it teach me about God the Father, the Son, or the Holy Spirit?
■ Is there a command for me to obey?
■ Is there an example for me to follow?
■ Is there a sin I should avoid?
■ Is there a promise I can claim? Is it conditional?
■ Is there a warning I should heed?

(*Note:* Every question may not apply to a given passage.)

—*Dick and Ann Honig, Berne, Indiana*

36
Using Dialogue
to Encourage Application

When the Apostle Paul arrived in a new city he would customarily meet with the religious leaders and "reason with them from the Scriptures" (Acts 17:2). In the original language, the verb in this phrase is *dialegomai,* from which we derive our word *dialogue.*

Paul would engage in question-and-answer discussions with the Jews. In response to the dialogue, some would be persuaded and would join Paul, and some would remain antagonistic. No matter what, the response always involved action. This is a characteristic of good dialogue: It always produces a response in attitude, action, or both.

Good dialogue requires diligent preparation by the leader. Like Paul, the leader must have studied and internalized the passage and applied its truths to his or her own life. He must have prepared questions in advance and be skilled in formulating extemporaneous questions in response to ideas and suggestions offered by the group. He must do as little talking as possible and prayerfully listen to group members, seeking to be sensitive to real needs which may be unspoken.

Application Through Dialogue

Properly guided through a Bible study, group members will arrive at an understanding of a Scripture passage as it relates to attitudes or behavior toward God, family members, our Christian friends, or those in our lives who do not yet know Christ as Savior and Lord. The dialogue leader can stimulate group members to apply biblical principles by asking questions that prompt individuals to discuss them and put them into action.

Here are some sample questions:

■ In your own words, how would you summarize the main truth in this passage?
■ Is there anything in your situation that is similar to the situation addressed in this passage?
■ How does the principle you have just stated apply to your situation?
■ Can you remember anything that has happened in your own life that might illustrate how this principle works out in reality?

■ How will you apply this truth or principle to a circumstance or person in your circle of influence this week?
■ Will you write down one commitment to God that you are willing to make regarding a change in attitude or behavior this week?
■ How can we pray with you that God will provide the resources you need this week to keep your commitment?
■ Will you take some time at our next meeting to share with us the results of the commitment you are making tonight?

—Tom Lovejoy, Associate Pastor of FLOCKS ministry, Grace Community Church, Sun Valley, California

37
How to Memorize Scripture

Are group members having difficulty memorizing Scripture? If so, try the following:

1. Ask God to give them a driving desire to memorize His Word.
2. Do a Bible study together that stresses the benefits of knowing God's Word.
3. Decide what to memorize. You might want to begin with a plan such as the *Topical Memory System* (NavPress). You can also select key verses from Bible studies and quiet times.
4. Before beginning to memorize the verse, have group members explain it in their own words. Make sure they understand its meaning.
5. Teach them to say the reference each time they repeat the verse, both at the beginning and the end. That way there will be one less person saying, "Somewhere in the Bible it says. . . ."
6. Repetition is the most productive method for memorizing. Engage as many of the senses as you can. Have group members read the verse out loud. Have them write it on an index card to carry with them. Sometimes it's helpful to write one phrase of the verse, or even one word, per card, like flashcards. Once group members have several verses under their belts, have them record the verses on a cassette tape to use for review. Which brings us to the next point.
7. Review, review, review. Have group members review a newly

learned verse daily for six weeks. Then they can move the verse card into a weekly review box. After another six weeks, they can move that same verse card into a monthly review box. Set aside one month to review all the verses learned that year.

—*Rebecca Livermore, San Angelo, Texas*

Why Memorize Scripture?
Use this study in your group to build convictions about the value of memorizing God's Word.

1. How can Scripture help you practice the principle found in Psalm 119:97,148?
2. According to Romans 12:2 and Colossians 3:2, how can memorizing Scripture change a person's life?
3. In what way can Scripture memory help you obey the commands found in Colossians 3:16 and 1 Peter 3:15?
4. In Matthew 4:1-11, how did Jesus demonstrate the importance of knowing the Word?
5. What does Philippians 4:8 tell us to think about? How can Scripture memory help us do that?
6. According to Psalm 119:11, how did David fight against sin in his life? In what practical way can you implement that strategy?

—*Navigator staff*

38
Integrating Scripture Memory with Application

I have hidden your word in my heart
that I might not sin against you. (Psalm 119:11)

Christian leaders have long used this passage to encourage believers to memorize Scripture. But in practice, many have not helped people to hide God's Word in their *hearts* so much as to hide it in their *minds*.
When the psalmist wrote about hiding Scripture in his heart, he

meant that he was depositing that truth in the center of his person.

Hiding God's Word in our hearts goes beyond reciting verses from memory. It is unfortunate that some Scripture memory techniques offer only the recitation approach: saying it over and over until it comes automatically.

Some people believe they are just not capable of memorizing Scripture: "I've tried; I just can't do it." Or "It's not my thing. I don't remember well." But those same people perform many daily tasks, often complicated ones, from memory. Perhaps this is because the tasks are directly related to their lifestyle.

Keeping this in mind, you can help the people in your group memorize Scripture effectively by relating the memory process to their lives. Here are some suggestions.

First, select Scripture verses that are relevant to the everyday lives of the believers in your group. For instance, as a member learns what it means to obey God's Word, he or she will find new opportunities to demonstrate to others at work or in recreation how his or her life is changing. An obedient Christian should be prepared to "give an answer" to people who ask about the changes they observe. So 1 Peter 3:15 is a good verse to memorize as the group starts out.

Second, complement the group's memorization process by teaching the passage in the group. Teaching the passage to be memorized helps members sift it through their minds, contemplating how it applies to them individually and in their roles as ambassadors for Christ. They must learn the contexts of the passages they memorize as well, in order to apply them to their lives correctly.

To help small-group participants learn the passages they are committing to memory and apply them to their lives, I've used the following schedule. Each week we devote about fifteen minutes of our group time to these discussions.

Week One
Group members memorize the selected passage and recite it during one of the three meetings that follow.

Week Two
As a group, identify the context of the memory verse. What is the author talking about in the passage where the verse is located?

Week Three
Discuss the focal point of the verse. Why is it included in this particular passage? How does it relate to the context of the passage?

Week Four
Apply the verse to life. How has the verse affected the thinking and lifestyle of the group members?

■ ■ ■

Once the group completes the four-week cycle, it is important to review previously learned verses each week.

The results of this approach to Scripture memory are encouraging—group members not only memorize Scripture, they hide God's Word in their hearts.

—Don DeJong, Northwest Regional Director, Churches Alive! ministry

39
How to Prepare and Do a Word Study

Preparation
Steps the leader should follow before the meeting:

1. Choose a word that is significant and occurs often enough in the Bible to be worth the group's time for study. Look at related forms of the word. For example: freedom/free; salvation/saved/save; ministry/minister; serve/servant.
2. Consult a concordance or topical Bible to locate all the passages in which the word occurs. Discover: How often does the word occur and where? Does the word appear to have the same meaning wherever it occurs or is it used in different ways by different authors?
3. Decide on some key passages for the group to investigate. Limit the amount of material.
4. Provide tools for the group to use—dictionaries, word books, and various translations of the Bible.

Procedures
Steps the leader should take during the meeting:

1. Announce the word to be studied and ask each member to write a one- or two-sentence definition in his or her own words. This should take three to four minutes.

2. Read or hand out a list of the key passages in which the word occurs, along with any study aids (listed above) that the group will use.
3. If your group is large, divide it into groups of two to four people. Each group should look up each reference in sequence and answer the following questions. This step should take about twenty to twenty-five minutes.

   ■ How is the word used and what does it mean in this passage? How does the context in which it appears help to define it?
   ■ As we look at each new reference, how does it further illuminate the meaning of the word? Is anything new added or emphasized? Is anything changed?
   ■ What do our reference tools add to our understanding of the word?
   ■ What are our conclusions about its meaning? How do these match or expand what we had written in the beginning?

Discussion
How the leader can help the group share and discuss their findings:

1. Have each person (or group) report their answers to these questions: What did you discover about this word? Why is it important?
2. Have a general discussion over these questions: As a result of your study, how would you define this word to someone who had no idea what it meant? Why is this word relevant to Christian belief and behavior? Allow fifteen to twenty minutes for this step.

—*From* Using the Bible in Groups *by Roberta Hestenes (Westminster Press, 1983)*

40
How to Write
Bible Study Material

Do you write your own Bible study guides? Here are some seasoned tips from Paul D. Stevens, teaching elder at Marineview Chapel, for writing personal study sections, group study materials, and group relational exercises.

PERSONAL STUDY SECTIONS

1. Vary the depth of your questions. Some questions will require reflection and continuing study—for these you may want to add, "If you are unable to answer this question now, come back to it later." For easier questions, try using a chart with fill-in sections.

Sometimes it's valuable to challenge more advanced students by suggesting an optional exercise: a hard interpretive question, a word study, or an examination of a parallel passage.

2. Avoid routine liturgical exhortations. Don't start every study with "Pray for the leading of the Holy Spirit." But do intersperse encouragements such as "Stop for a moment to ask God to show you how this fits into your life."

3. Test your study by doing it yourself. Time it (it shouldn't take more than an hour). Then ask someone who has never studied the passage to do it and tell you what questions were vague or irrelevant.

4. Avoid yes or no questions and those with too obvious answers. But avoid overchallenging and thus discouraging beginning learners.

5. Resist the temptation to "rig the truth." Don't lead your group into making your discovery, or leave them asking, "What was the writer driving at?" Instead, help people make fresh discoveries for themselves.

6. Make sure every personal study leads to personal action. Build into the study a challenge to "do the doctrine."

Group Study Materials

Assume that everyone is doing personal study. Build into the study at least one specific contribution from personal study. Here are some ideas:

■ Divide the passage into sections and have each member share in one minute what he or she learned from that section. This will need to be set up the previous week, but the whole passage will be surveyed briefly and everyone shares.

■ Build into the personal study a specific point that will be shared with the group, such as, "The one prayer request I have for this group as a result of studying this passage is. . . ."

■ Ask one member in advance to teach the passage in ten to fifteen minutes at the beginning of the meeting.

Group Relational Exercises

These exercises focus on applying the passage to our relationships as a group. Particular passages may suggest exercises in the following areas:

■ Affirming one another's gifts.
■ Communicating feelings and experiences.

■ Prayer for personal hurts and hopes.
■ Developing a Christian concept of leadership, order, servant-hood, plurality, inner authority, and freedom.

When writing relational exercises, spell out specific guidelines. For example, "Make sure everyone shares his viewpoint on this"; "Limit this part of the discussion to twenty minutes"; "No one is allowed to communicate a negative while we are affirming strengths"; "Make sure no one's prayer request is ignored. Write them all down."

—Leadership 100 *(1983). Used by permission.*

Prayer

41
Take the Fear Out of Group Prayer

Remember the first time you prayed out loud in a group of people? If you're like most of us, you were probably pretty nervous. Most likely your hands were sweaty, your throat got dry, and your mind raced ahead, trying to think of the right words to pray.

It's important to remember how you felt, because there might be someone in your small group who feels the same way you once did. For them, prayer time is not a wonderful, intimate time of fellowship with the Father; it's a stress-filled time that ties their stomachs into knots.

Fear of praying out loud could keep someone from returning to your small group. To make sure this doesn't happen, what can you do, as a leader, to ease prayer anxiety and help your group experience the joy of praying in a group setting? Here are some suggestions.

Never force someone to pray. Prayer should be a voluntary response from the heart. When praying together as a group, it's important to let people know it's okay if they do not pray out loud. Encourage them to join with the group in silent prayer. Avoid going around the circle in order, each person taking a turn. Even if someone has the option to pass, he or she may feel awkward doing so.

Don't unexpectedly single out someone to pray. If you want to ask a particular person to pray, ask permission prior to the meeting. Let the other group members know that the person praying has volunteered so they won't be worried that one evening you will call on them to pray.

Teach about prayer. Discuss on a regular basis what prayer is and how important it is. Communicate to your group that prayer does not consist of eloquent and inspiring phrases, but rather heartfelt communication. Encourage openness and honesty in prayer, and downplay the urge to sound "spiritual" in front of others.

Focus on prayer requests. Allow sufficient time for prayer requests. Many people who would not feel comfortable verbalizing their prayers are willing to talk about what's going on in their lives. Sharing prayer requests gives them an opportunity to participate in the group prayer time without feeling threatened.

Include silent prayer times. Some of the most encouraging prayer times I have experienced in a group setting have been times of silence. No one is worrying about what to say. Everyone is focused on the prayer requests at hand. Silent prayer can enrich and support group members when everyone is focused on specific needs and requests.

Use word and sentence prayers. Every so often, structure your prayer time around single word or sentence prayers. This helps people get comfortable with praying in a group. You can open up a prayer time by asking for single words of thanks or single sentences praising God's attributes.

Pray as a group. Repeating a prayer line for line after the leader can be a unifying experience. You can also read a psalm together as prayer.

Guide the prayers. Leaders can guide a prayer time by focusing the group on one topic at a time and moving them to the next topic after a sufficient time. This method is less threatening to newer group members because it is structured, and they don't have to think about including all the requests they've heard into their prayers. A second benefit for prayer-shy group members: Prayers focused on a single topic tend to be shorter.

Strengthen private prayer lives. The more a person grows in his private prayer life, the more likely he is to grow in his desire and ability to pray in a public setting. Ask group members to commit to praying for specific prayer requests throughout the week. This will help them mature in their private prayer lives.

Be a model. The most important thing a small-group leader can do is model an authentic prayer life for his small group. People are quick to recognize honesty and humility. If they see a leader open his heart to the Lord without regard to how he sounds in front of others, they will be more likely to follow that example.

—*Mark Whelchel, Las Vegas, Nevada*

42
The Focus of Group Prayer

There are at least three dimensions of a small group's life together that are vital subjects for dialogue with God. The first is the dimension of our life *when we are gathered.* Here our concerns relate to the effectiveness of the time that we have together and to the role that Christ has among us. By His Holy Spirit, it is Christ's delight to bind us together (Romans 15:5-7) and to nurture us in His truth (John 16:12-15). We might talk with Him about the elements of our time which will move us toward His goals—about our desire to be taught by His Spirit through our study of Scripture, about our openness in sharing with one another, and about helping us to affirm our unity as well as to appreciate and encourage our God-given diversity.

We might thank Him for His presence and role among us, and praise Him for those attributes for which we are especially grateful. We can ask for guidance, healing, vision, and greater love for one another. Our chief concern should be that we will have open, teachable hearts so that we can hear and respond to the movement of the Spirit among us. Our life together is important to us, but it is even more important to God.

The second dimension of a small group's life about which we should approach God is our life *when we are scattered.* Beyond the meeting itself, each member of a small group has responsibilities, relationships, personal concerns, and ministry opportunities. In this dimension we can be supporting each other as individuals in our struggles with sin, in our disciplined obedience to God's call, in our sensitivity to the unavoidable world which surrounds each one, and in our outreach into the world which is avoidable but to which God sends us.

We might pray that God would empower each of us to be a center of His grace and love when we are apart. Praying in this dimension might come as a response to our sharing of personal concerns during the small-group time. It is a very concrete way of communicating love to one another and of standing with each other even when we are apart.

A third dimension goes beyond ourselves to *the wider world*, including both fellow Christians and those who do not yet know Christ.

Here we might pray for specific struggles or concerns, but also for the long-term maturity, wisdom, perseverance, healing and growth of the Body of Christ (see Paul's prayers in Colossians 1:9-14; Ephesians 1:15-20; 1 Thessalonians 3:9-13; 2 Thessalonians 1:3,11-12). We might want to pray specifically for those with whom we would want to share Christ or for those who we know are struggling to make a decision. It is exciting to pray for world problems, for rulers and governments, and for issues of justice. God's concerns are far broader than ours and praying for the world increases our vision.

Praying in each of these three dimensions actually contributes in a different way to the life of a small group. Praying for the time when we are gathered binds us together. Praying for each other when we are scattered builds a sense of support and empowers us in our individual walks. Praying for the world beyond us guards our fellowship from becoming ingrown.

—*Stephen A. Hayner, President, Intervarsity Fellowship*

43
Helpful Hints for Small-Group Prayer

Some people feel anxious about praying aloud. Others are comfortable praying aloud, but don't feel comfortable about sharing their deepest needs for prayer.

If members of your group are timid about praying because they don't know the group well or because they think their prayers are "dumb," start simply. Assure the group that one-sentence prayers please God just as well as elaborate ones. Begin by thanking the Lord for one thing and encourage each member of the group to thank Him for one thing also: "Father, I thank You for my family. . . . Lord, I thank You for the health You've given me. . . ." Hearing one's own voice in prayer, and knowing that it is pleasing and acceptable to God, builds confidence and an increasing awareness of God's presence with a person as he prays.

If the members of your group share only the prayer needs of their friends and relatives and none of their own, perhaps they need some encouragement to share their own deepest needs for prayer. Choose a passage from Scripture such as Colossians 1:10-12, Philippians 1:9-11, or Ephesians 1:15-19. Use the passage as a pattern for intercession, and pray through the passage for each member of the group. This can be effective during the group's meeting and during the week between meetings.

By using Colossians 1:9-12, for instance, you might pray that Sue would bear fruit for the Lord in her work, grow in her knowledge of Him in her study, and be strengthened with endurance and patience in her family and home. God may use these prayers to bring to Sue's mind specific needs in these areas she would like to share.

Scripture reveals the Lord's work in the many areas of our lives. It also shows us where we fall short of His glory. Praying through these passages helps us to acknowledge His power of transformation in our lives and teaches us to appreciate and rely on the prayer support of others.

—*Navigator staff*

44
Six Ways to Pray with Your Group

If your group spends more time talking about prayer than actually praying, or if the prayers sound too much like "gimme" lists, try some of the following ideas.

Alphabet Soup
Call out a letter of the alphabet. As people in the group think of an attribute or aspect of God's nature beginning with that letter, have them say the word or phrase and then briefly praise God for that character quality. For example, if you say "T," a group member might respond with "Trustworthy: Lord, thank You that I can trust You." Another says, "Tenderness: God, I praise You for Your tender loving care." To keep things moving, the leader mentions another letter frequently.

The Name Above All Names
Compile a list of the different forms of the name *Jehovah* and what they mean. Hand out copies to the group and ask them to spend a few minutes meditating on the names. Invite each member to share a name that is particularly meaningful to him or her and to turn it into a short prayer. The person praying might say, "Father, You are Jehovah-Jireh, the Lord who provides. Thank You for providing me with a person to talk to this week when I was lonely but too afraid to admit it." (One source for a list of the names of God is *The Hallelujah Factor* by Jack Taylor, Broadman Press.)

Sign-in Prayer Requests
If your time is limited, a sign-in system can help the group spend less time explaining prayer needs and more time praying. Have a sheet of paper ready and ask people to write down their requests as they arrive or before the meeting begins. During prayer time, read each item aloud and ask someone to pray about it.

Prayer Shuffle
A variation on the sign-in sheet is to have members note requests on index cards. If you have many needs to pray for, divide into groups of three. Shuffle the cards and hand out a few to each group.

Global Perspective
Invite a missionary family to your group meeting to share their slides or a video. Lead the group in praying for the specific needs they mention during their presentation. If no missionaries are available, create awareness of world needs through video. Tape television programs that feature cultural issues or conditions. Check local TV listings for National Geographic specials, talk show topics, or programs about foreign countries. Use short clips to stimulate discussion and prayer.

Community Concerns
Clip articles from your newspaper about local issues or people who have specific needs. Use the clippings as a basis for intercession either with the group as a whole or in pairs.
—*Corinne Hamada Holmquist, Ashville, North Carolina*

45
Worship in Small Groups

PRAYER PATTERNED ON THE PSALMS
Select an appropriate praise psalm (such as Psalms 66, 93, 98, 100, 105, 111) to use in one of the following ways:

- Pray a verse in unison, then pause to let individuals add their own thoughts and praises before continuing to the next.
- After sharing, select a few verses of a praise psalm to paraphrase, building on the shared experiences of the group. Read several of these paraphrases as prayers.
- Select praise verses from the psalms for memorization by the group.
- Discuss a psalm in depth, exploring the portrait of God it gives and the works of God that have led to praise, relating it to our lives today.
- Write a modern-day psalm together, focusing on a particular theme (God's goodness, power, blessing).

SPONTANEOUS PRAYER
Spontaneous prayer may be short and interjectory—simply a "Thank You, Lord." It may also be a longer expression of praise and thanksgiv-

SMALL-GROUP IDEAS / PRAYER

ing. Often groups will not develop this practice because it seems unusual. Yet spontaneous prayers help each person find sensitivity to the Lord's presence that will carry over into daily life.

To help the group feel more comfortable with spontaneous prayer and praise:

1. Talk over the idea as a group, freely discussing any hesitation members might have.
2. Plan to have spontaneous prayer for two sessions of the group meeting, encouraging members to lead the group in praise when they feel the Lord's presence in a special way. At first this will seem artificial, but it may lead to a true expression of worship and praise.
3. Select a praise leader for each session, asking him or her to be sensitive to times when the group shares an experience that naturally leads to praise. After several weeks, no praise leader should be needed: All members will be sensitized to the Lord's presence.

—*Taken from* Sixty-Nine Ways to Start a Study Group *by Lawrence O. Richards (Zondervan, 1973)*

46
The Prayer Sandwich

"Pastor Wes Andre originally developed the Prayer Sandwich concept for our small group in Regina, Saskatchewan," says Joyce Phillips. "It has been exciting to see how God has honored it."

First slice of bread: We enter into God's presence and make our hearts right with Him through prayers of confession, thanksgiving, and praise.

The filling: We read aloud specific Scripture verses the Holy Spirit has laid on our hearts during the week. It's surprising how these verses, coming from group members who are not aware of what verses others will be reading, confirm each other. After sharing scriptures, the group leader pulls the verses together into one or two lessons that the Holy Spirit is impressing on him or her. If he or she doesn't feel led to do this, it's okay, since the Holy Spirit will have already spoken through the verses themselves.

Top slice of bread: We finish the "sandwich" with prayers of supplication and intercession. Now that we have made our hearts right with God through confession, thanksgiving, and praise, and have listened to His Word, we can present our needs to Him.

The Prayer Sandwich works because it is based on biblical principles and gives God's Spirit an opportunity to speak to us through His Word. The things people learn during the week not only meet individual needs but strengthen the bonds between group members. Members find themselves looking forward to each week's gathering, eager to learn what the Lord will say to them as a group and as individuals.

—*Mrs. Joyce Phillips, Saskatchewan, Canada*

47
"Prayer Triplets" in Action

I introduced the idea of using a prayer card to the men at my church's Friday morning prayer breakfast. The goal is to develop "prayer triplets" who covenant to pray daily for each other and for unsaved friends and relatives. To use this card,

1. Find two prayer partners who will agree to meet weekly to pray for nonChristians.
2. Have each person list on your card the names of three unbelievers for whom he'd like to pray. On their cards, write the names of three people you know.
3. Pray daily for the nine people listed on your card.
4. Meet with your prayer partners weekly for prayer. Include personal prayer requests as needed.

It's been exciting to see people pray regularly for unsaved relatives and friends, encouraged by the fact that two other people were praying for them too! This prayer ministry has expanded our church's interest in evangelism.

—*Claude A. VanAndel, Muskegon, Michigan*

48
Cures for Humdrum Prayer Times

Behind most people's frustration with group prayer is a lack of variety. Week after week, it's the same. "Let's go around the room and share requests. . . . Okay, let's pray now." And back around the room you go again. Resolve not to use the same prayer method twice in a row, then try the following ideas to bring freshness to group prayer:

■ After one person shares her requests, ask the *person on her right* to pray briefly for her. Move through the group this way. After everyone's requests have been brought before the Lord, close with five or ten minutes of sentence prayers that focus on praise and worship.

■ Devote all but the last five minutes of your prayer time to *praise, thanksgiving*, and talking to God about the Bible study you just did. During the last five minutes, let group members pair up, share a prayer request, and briefly pray for each other.

■ Share *answers* to prayer. Whenever answers come, stop right then and give God thanks. Answered prayer and verbalized gratefulness bring energy and enthusiasm to our prayer lives.

■ Vary your prayer *posture*. Kneel, stand in a circle and hold hands, raise hands in praise, etc.

■ Let *music* enhance your times of worship. There are many worship choruses that can "get you in the mood" for expressing adoration and praise. One group leader used music to lead her group through several prayer transitions. One worship song led the group into adoration, another set the stage for several minutes of silent confession, another led into thanksgiving, and a fourth chorus prepared the group for bringing their requests before God.

■ Schedule *extended times* for prayer. Meet for bagels and coffee on a Saturday morning, then spend an hour or two in group prayer. If your busy schedules make it difficult to get together outside of your regular meeting time, devote every fourth (or sixth, etc.) meeting to prayer.

■ Keep a *prayer file* with ideas for varying group prayer.

■ Set *guidelines for sharing* requests. You may need to limit each person to two minutes. Some groups limit prayer requests to those involving group members or their immediate family. Another excellent guideline is to prohibit problem-solving. If Sam has the perfect solution to Hank's dilemma, let him discuss it after the group dismisses.

—*Navigator staff*

49
Sharing Prayer Requests

To cut down on the time your group spends talking about prayer requests so that you can spend more time praying, consider using these methods to share prayer requests.

■ Give everyone an index card to write down their prayer concerns for the week and have them exchange cards with another member of the group. For the following week (or until the next time you meet), you will pray for the specific requests on your card. On the other side of the card, you can write the memory verse for the upcoming week.

■ At the beginning of each month, pass around a master calendar on which group members can write down important events (birthdays, anniversaries, tests, doctor appointments, etc.). Make copies of the calendars for everyone in the group so they can pray for these events on the appropriate day.

—*Kyrie Nilson, Bellingham, Washington*

50
Plugging into the Source

It's common to see people relaxing by plugging earphones into a cassette player. They know the benefits of tuning out the world and tuning into something soothing like music. So why not teach this concept to your small-group friends who are beginning to depend on God daily in His Word?

Since many people like to keep diaries, I have developed a Bible study format that would coax Christians to use their Bible concordance. You could use this during a group outing as an individual exercise, then have people come back and share what they have learned.

Encourage your group members to use this method in their daily quiet time.

Date:

Rewind: List key activities and emotions you've encountered today or are anticipating tomorrow. Then circle the one you feel the need to seek God's advice on.

Label: Give your feelings and experiences one-word labels. Check your Bible reference guide or concordance for Scriptures to read on these topics. Or look up a person in the Bible who experienced something similar.

Fast forward: Jot down the references here. Then the texts.

Record: Write the verse or promise you would like to believe God will fulfill concerning this area.

Play: Continue to "play on" with your life, but think of a practical way you can apply God's truth to your situation or attitude. Write it down. How can you remind yourself of this application in the future?

End side one with prayer.

—*Corinne Hamada Holmquist, Asheville, North Carolina*

51
"I Always Forget to Pray"

It's time for prayer requests. Everyone takes out prayer notebooks and diligently records requests as they are shared. But you are thinking, *I always write down these requests, but I never remember to pray for them once we leave our small-group meeting. Am I the only one who struggles with this?*

Rest assured, you are not alone. Here are a few ideas to help you and your group members pray for one another throughout the week.

■ *Call for volunteers*. As each prayer request is voiced, ask for one or two volunteers to agree in prayer during the week.

Members will likely respond quickest if they've experienced a similar situation, so draw out volunteers with questions like, "Has anyone had a similar problem on the job?" or "Who else knows what it's like to carry a burden for an unsaved parent?"

■ *Pair up.* Assign prayer partners for a month (draw names out of a hat, etc.). When Jim shares a request, he knows his prayer partner for the month, Dave, will be praying for him in the days ahead.

■ *Respond immediately to urgent requests.* If someone is facing serious surgery, for example, ask group members to lay hands on him or her while someone prays.

■ *Conduct a prayer vigil.* Cover a crisis with continuous prayer. Perhaps someone is facing a difficult meeting with a disgruntled employee, or exploratory surgery, or a critical exam. Ask group members to sign up to pray for half-hour intervals (or ten minutes, etc.) during the critical time period.

■ *Vary your methods.* Any method loses effectiveness if used exclusively. Brainstorm in your group some additional ideas for staying disciplined in praying for one another.

—Esther Bailey, Phoenix, Arizona

52
Proclaim a Group Fast

Food, fun, and fellowship are all important parts of small-group life— but when's the last time your group added fasting to that list?

Fasting, perhaps the most neglected of all the disciplines, was practiced in both the Old and New Testaments. Even Jesus spent extended time in fasting and prayer.

If your small group is involved in a spiritual battle or facing a major decision such as a change in leadership, fasting can help your group determine God's will (Judges 20:26-28, Acts 14:23).

Or consider corporate fasting during times of crisis. (See 2 Chronicles 20:1-3, Esther 4:3, and Jonah 3:3-9.) Recently, a member of our women's Bible study reached a crisis point in her marriage and decided to leave her husband. Our group was grieved and agreed to pray and fast for the restoration of her marriage. Although she declared she didn't want to try to work things out with her husband, within one week of our day of fasting her marriage was restored.

Others have found through fasting a release of heavy burdens, healing, increased righteousness, guidance, and strength.

Here are some considerations if you'd like to try a corporate fast in your small group.

A Few Weeks Before the Fast
- Bring up the topic in your small-group meeting. Be prepared to address questions and concerns.
- Encourage those who've never fasted to try a partial fast (fruit, vegetables, and water) at least a week before the group fast.
- Encourage those whose medical conditions prohibit fasting (e.g., pregnant women) to bring a sack lunch and come anyway.
- Begin praying that God will prepare each person's heart.

The Day of the Fast
- Start with a Bible study on fasting.
- Spend time in worship to help people focus on God.
- Devote extended time to prayer. Pray for specific needs in the church. (Ask your pastor for requests ahead of time.) Pray for missionaries and for other parts of the world. Pray for each other. Break into groups of two or three for part of the time. Devote at least an hour to solitary personal prayer and Bible reading.
- Keep plenty of water (and perhaps juice) on hand.
- Come together at the end of the day for sharing.

■ ■ ■

People associate fasting with deprivation. But your small-group members are more likely to find that a day of fasting, fellowship, worship, and prayer leaves them feeling refreshed and filled, not deprived.

—*Rebecca Livermore, San Angelo, Texas*

79

Fellowship

53
The Small-Group Mix

After you have been in a group for several weeks, it may be time to take stock of your relationships with others in the group. This can be a valuable exercise, for our relationships in a small group often mirror our relationships with people in general. Think back through your small-group experience as you answer these questions.

1. What sort of group member are you? Check the descriptive phrases below that best describe how you act in your small group.

   ☐ Shy   ☐ Passive   ☐ Summarizing
   ☐ Overtalkative   ☐ Looking on   ☐ Bored
   ☐ Argumentative   ☐ Hostile   ☐ Enthusiastic
   ☐ Witty   ☐ Silent   ☐ Fearful
   ☐ Aggressive   ☐ Theorizing   ☐ Peacemaker
   ☐ Hidden agenda   ☐ Leading   ☐ Baffled

2. Why do you suppose you function this way?
3. Which roles do you play in the small group?
4. How does your presence benefit the group?
5. What are the potential problems?
6. What aspect of your behavior in the group would you like to change? Why?
7. How can you do this?
8. How do you think others in this group view you?
9. Do you have problems relating to anyone in the group? Why?
10. What can you do to improve the relationships?
11. How would you rate your honesty?
12. How would you rate your acceptance of others?
13. If you dared to be totally honest with one other person, what would you share?
14. From your relationships in the group, what have you learned about your relationships to your family? Your friends? Your colleagues?

—Taken from Small Group Evangelism *by Richard Peace, copyright 1985. Used by permission of InterVarsity Press.*

54
Fifteen Questions to Help You Get Better Acquainted

1. What is your favorite Sunday afternoon pastime and why?
2. What hobby was most enjoyable in your teens?
3. What is the one thing that gives you the most satisfaction?
4. What is one thing you are good at doing?
5. Who is the most influential person in your life?
6. When you are fifty, what do you hope to be doing?
7. What three things do (did) you most like about your father? About your mother?
8. What one thing did you dislike about your parents?
9. What is the most frightening experience you've ever had?
10. When did God become more than a word to you?
11. Describe your ideal house and how you would furnish it.
12. If you knew you could not fail, and money was no problem, what one thing would you like to do in the next five or ten years?
13. When and how did you first meet your spouse? What do you most remember about that time?
14. What is one thing you worried about this past week?
15. What is one thing you are proud of about yourself?

—*Dr. Donald Reed, Saint John's Lutheran Church, Bakersfield, California*

55
Basic Small-Group Interaction

LISTENING

Listening is hard work. If you're not listening hard, you communicate that you don't care and you can't help.

Do not interrupt another person with your voice, your body movement, your eyes, your gesture, or your lack of concentration.

Do not interrupt mentally. Do not plan what you are going to say when the speaker is finished. Listen.

Listen to *intent* as well as *content.* The deepest level of communication is nonverbal. Understand what's being felt as well as spoken. Hear every nuance of tone, meaning, accent, body movement, posture, and eye contact.

SPEAKING

Be personal. Use the first person singular—"I."

Don't preach! Preachy words are: *we, should, ought, everyone, all Christians, no* (real) *Christian, all, no one, all of us, everybody.*

Talk unpretentiously, on a level of your own personal experience. Don't substitute theories, sermons, great books, or long passages of Scripture (unless they have helped you personally).

Talk about "what," not "why." Don't probe. Unless you are a psychotherapist, leave the analysis to someone else. Point to what you see or feel in the here and now.

PERSONAL SHARING

Be as honest about where you are not in the Christian life as where you are. Let the other person know that it's okay for him or her to struggle, to be human, to fail, and to be vulnerable.

You are "Exhibit A" that God can work in anyone's life, that He has an investment in frail humanity, and that He can change people. Don't worry, you won't make God look bad. And remember, you have yet to walk on water!

Avoid giving advice. Even if you are asked, give advice only as a last resort. The secret is to help people find their own answers. Share your common identity if you have had a similar problem.

DEALING WITH PAIN

Always acknowledge when another person is hurting. Never ignore crying or make excuses for it, and don't allow the group to do it either. Show that you care—you do not always need to speak to do this. Touch an arm or shoulder, hug him or her (if you are free enough), take a hand, lend a handkerchief. Verbally or silently, pray for him or her on the spot. You may feel led to ask, "How can I (we) pray right now? . . . Help you? . . . Support you?"

MAKING PROMISES

Make specific promises and covenants: "Bob, I promise you that. . . ." "Bob, I covenant with you. . . ."

Do not require others to promise you anything unless they really want to. You may, of course, enlist their help, support, and prayers. The great relationships of life between God and people, and between people and people, are sealed with promises.

—From an unpublished pamphlet, Enabling a Small Group, *Bel Air Presbyterian Church, Los Angeles, California. Used by permission.*

56
Glad You Asked

Building relationships is a goal of every small group. This requires sharing at increasing levels of intimacy. Mixer questions are one way to encourage this, not just in the early stages of getting acquainted, but throughout the group's life cycle.

Most small-group leaders pour considerable time and effort into writing Bible study discussion questions, but rarely give much thought to mixers. I suggest writing a variety of mixer questions for each of the following categories.

- *History-giving:* How did your family celebrate Christmas when you were in grade school?
- *Personal values:* Describe three characteristics for an ideal friend.
- *Future dreams:* What would you like to be doing in five years?
- *Affirmation:* What are two of your strongest skills?
- *Current events:* Tell us three things that happened to you today.

After writing several questions for each category, consider several different formats for sharing. You might divide your group into pairs or threesomes. You might separate men from women. You can write different questions on slips of paper, then have each group member draw one and answer it in front of the whole group. As you try different formats you will learn which works best with your small group. Just take into account your time limit, the level of intimacy in the group, and whether you want to help others bond with only a few or with the whole group.

—David Gschwend, Pastor of South Hills Community Church in San Jose, California

57
Encouraging Words

"A word of encouragement does wonders!" (Proverbs 12:25). Betty Robertson suggests two ways her Bible study groups have given positive feedback to each other:

Bombardment: Each week, choose one person in the group to bombard with positive comments. Speak directly to the individual: "Sue, I appreciate your quiet, gentle spirit."

Web of Love: The members of the group sit in a circle. The leader has a ball of yarn. He wraps the yarn around his finger and tosses the ball to someone in the group. He expresses his appreciation to that person, who in turn loops the yarn around his finger and then throws the ball to someone he wants to affirm. This continues until a large "web" of love connects the group.

—*Betty Robertson, Bethany, Oklahoma*

58
Icebreakers to Help Warm Up Your Group

Use these suggestions to learn more personal information about the people in your group or to break the ice in a new group:

The Four Quaker Questions (for cold winter meetings)
1. Where were you living between the ages of seven and twelve, and what were winters like then?
2. How was your home heated during that time?
3. What was the center of warmth in your life when you were a child? (It could be a place in the house, a time of year, a person.)
4. When did God become a "warm" Person to you, and how did it happen?

Talk About Some Important Memories
■ The first time I became aware of God's love
■ The first time I liked a member of the opposite sex

- The first time I tried to dance
- The first time I was afraid
- The first time I received an answer to prayer

—James P. Young, Escondido, California

59
Breaking "Small-Group Ice"

The first minutes of small-group meetings are vital. Good icebreakers can cut away social barriers and promote open sharing throughout the rest of the meeting. Some of our most successful icebreakers have been to ask every person to complete one of the following statements:

- If I knew I couldn't fail, I'd try. . . .
- One lesson I've learned the hard way is. . . .
- Some of the best advice I was given is. . . .
- One unfulfilled dream of mine is. . . .
- You would know me better if you knew that I. . . .
- More than anything, I would like to be remembered as a person who. . . .
- If I could have a five-minute face-to-face meeting with Jesus Christ, I would talk about. . . .
- Given one day to do anything I'd like, with no economic constraints, I would choose to. . . .

—Glenn T. Murphy, Minister of Discipleship and Outreach, Millington Baptist Church, Millington, New Jersey

60
Eight Weeks of Icebreakers

Come September, many groups resume meeting after a summer break. Often there are new members among the old. Or perhaps all your group members are new to each other. Here are eight weeks' worth of icebreaker questions to help you get better acquainted.

1. What is the scariest thing you ever had to do? In retrospect, are you glad you did it or do you have regrets?
2. What was the last thing you saw someone do that really impressed you? Explain.
3. What did you wear to your last costume party?
4. If you had to eat the same food for dinner for an entire week, what would it be?
5. What was your favorite book (or story) when you were a child? What did you like about it?
6. What is your favorite room in your home? Why?
7. What ability do you wish you had that you don't? Why?
8. If money was no object, where would you like to have a vacation home?

61
Fun, Food, and Family

Life Friends
My singles' Bible study enjoyed the following activities:

N.A.P.L. (Not Another Pot Luck): We met at church or in homes and brought a favorite food—enough to feed three people. At the door, each person was given two numbers: One corresponded to a group of three people, and the other to a food dish. Once the music started, everyone had to find the food dish and two other people who had the same number. When the music stopped, everyone had two friends to eat dinner with and three kinds of food. Once, my group ended up with two desserts and a vegetable!

T.I.H.I.R.F. (This Is How I Really Feel): We discussed current issues, problems, etc., and talked honestly about what we felt, knowing that others would keep what we said confidential.

Y.N.K. (You'll Never Know): We didn't know until we arrived at the church if we would be bowling, playing board games, or something else. The spontaneity was great.

—*An anonymous* Discipleship Journal *reader from South Holland, Illinois*

Small-Group Gourmets
Singles' potlucks have earned a bad reputation, partly because of the overabundance of fast-food fried chicken and supermarket potato salad.

Libba Narron's singles' group found ways to transform the lowly potluck into "gourmet grab bags" by focusing on themes each month. Some of their successes:

- **Amish country picnic.** Meet in a local park and bring food that did not require electricity to prepare.
- **Trip down Memory Lane.** Bring baby pictures and make a favorite childhood dish. During dinner, share special childhood memories.
- **Sand and sea.** Play beach music. Bring food in the shape of something found at the beach. One diner brought a cake perched on a scuba fin with a can of whipped cream in the ankle strap.

—*Libba Narron, Greensboro, North Carolina*

MARKING MILESTONES
When a newly wed couple joined our small group, each member brought an inexpensive but useful gift for their new home. It took about fifteen minutes for the couple to open the gifts, was a great icebreaker, and allowed plenty of time for fellowship, Bible study, and prayer.
—*Jeannie Jones, Davenport, Iowa*

Editor's note: Jeannie's idea sparked some creative ideas from the *Discipleship Journal* team. June Whitely, *Discipleship Journal* fulfillment director, suggested honoring newlyweds or new home owners in your small group with a "pounding" in which each group member brings a pound of something—flour, butter, potatoes, etc.—for the celebrants. *Discipleship Journal* editor, Susan Maycinik, suggested giving small gifts for other milestones, such as earning a degree, having a baby, or buying a house. Present the milestoners with an advice book in which each group member writes words of wisdom, humorous or profound, to prepare the honorees for their big step in life.

62
On the Hot Seat

Have the group members bring either a photograph or a piece of paper on which they have drawn a picture to represent themselves. Staple each picture to a bulletin board and set it up where each member can see it.

Then place a chair at the front of the group and hand a dart to each person. The object is to toss the darts (one at a time!) at the bulletin board. Whoever's picture it lands on must sit on the "hot seat" up front. For the next ten minutes the group may ask that person any questions they want, keeping in mind two guidelines:

1. The person on the hot seat may plead the Fifth Amendment to any question.
2. No one may ask a question that involves answering by naming another person in an embarrassing way (e.g., Who gave you your first kiss?)

A few sample questions group members might ask: What was your most embarrassing moment? How did you feel the first time you were asked for a date—or did the asking? What is one of the happiest moments of your life?

People are always hesitant at first, whether the group is new or has been meeting for a while. But by the end of the session everyone's hoping the dart will land on their picture next!

—*Kent Wilson, Monument, Colorado*

63
Plan a Small-Group Escape

Does your small group need a booster shot? A small-group retreat might be what you're looking for.

Last spring our small group decided to escape to the mountains for a weekend, along with spouses and children. Some of us camped, others stayed in a motel. Some of us water-skied while others canoed, hiked, fished, and swam. We also spent time in serious discussion. Even though we've studied, prayed, and played together for years, this experience offered us new insights into who we are as families and renewed our appreciation of our unique friendships.

Choose a destination. Allow people to voice their dislikes, then choose a destination that everyone is willing to try. It's best to choose a setting that offers a variety of accommodations—campsites, cabins, motels, etc.

Keep your plans simple. Do discuss some activities you'd like to participate in—after all, some of them will require bringing sports equipment, etc. But allow plenty of time to just hang out together as families and individuals. Don't forget to plan for both good and bad weather.

Try one or two of the following activities to make your retreat memorable:

- **Theme for a day.** For example, begin the day with a devotional based on the parable of the mustard seed in Matthew 17:20-21. Give each person a mustard seed to carry in his pocket during the day. Include mustard in your lunch and dinner menus. In the evening, center your Bible discussion on faith.
- **Sunrise worship service.** Include a celebration of the Lord's Supper.
- **Time capsule.** Fill a shoe box with memorabilia from the weekend—the fishing line that pulled in the "big one," a seashell you found on the beach, etc. Include either a notebook or cassette tape of which you've taken turns recording events of the retreat. Set a date, perhaps in a year, to open the box together and reminisce.
- **The blessing game.** Try this as your weekend retreat is drawing to a close. In this version of "Spin the Bottle," the person at whom the bottle points shares some blessing received during the weekend.

—Betty Johnson, Parker, Colorado

64
A Blessing Exercise
(When Terminating Your Group)

Before a group disbands, it is important that there be healthy closure. Jacob told the angel, "I will not let you go until you bless me." When your group discontinues (as every group will sooner or later), you are, in fact, letting go of one another. Some of the ways you might "bless" one another include:

1. Prayer. Each member of the group might offer a special prayer for each of the others, such as, "My prayer for you is . . . ," or "I ask that God grant you. . . ."

2. Forgiveness. In some ways a blessing is a way of saying, "Maybe we have disappointed each other. Maybe we have not met each other's expectations. And I let you go so that you are free." This might require forgiving old wrongs and putting your house in order.

3. Encouragement and affirmation. Often groups terminate because members are beginning to wrestle with and respond to new calls. Part of the blessing is to help people explore these new callings—to help people make decisions and take the next step. They need to move on in their journey with your affirmation and encouragement.

—Pastor Charles Olsen, Arcadia Presbyterian Church, Arcadia, California

65
Fostering Fun

The following activity, designed to strengthen group relationships, will work equally well for Sunday school classes, small groups, or retreats.

1. Divide your group into teams of three or four people.
2. Give each team a bucket of tinker toys, Legos, or building blocks, and tell them to construct something that represents their team. They have ten minutes to finish their "team masterpiece."
3. Have each team explain their creation and answer the following questions:

   ■ What did you learn from this experience?
   ■ What can we learn about each other by doing something fun together?
   ■ How does having fun affect newcomers to the group?
   ■ What other activities could foster fun in the group?

4. Lead in a closing prayer something like this: "Thank You for fun, Lord. Thanks for laughter, the best medicine. Thank You for making our hearts merrier and our relationships stronger. We pray that our fun activities would bring glory to You, and maybe even a giggle or two. In Jesus' name. Amen."

—Clark Cothern, Adrian, Michigan

66
How to Promote Fellowship in Your Group

Most leaders would agree that interaction among group members, as well as between leaders and group members, is vital if your group is to go beyond the lecture/memorization phase of learning. But that doesn't just happen. It's usually up to the group leader to get the fellowship fires burning before the group session begins.

The following activities are designed to encourage that atmosphere of warmth, acceptance, and sharing among group members. Select or adapt one of these activities to begin your small group session. If you think some coffee and donuts might help, bring them along, too!

Who's who? Have everyone write about a brief, humorous incident from his or her childhood. Collect the papers and read the contents aloud without naming the writers. After each one is read, ask group members to guess who wrote it.

Photo gallery: Ask members to pull a picture from their purse or wallet and share it with the group (who it is, why it is significant, etc.).

Quotables: Usually someone has several old *Reader's Digest* magazines around. In advance, cut out the "Quotable Quotes" page from several of these. During your fellowship time pass the pages around and have members clip off with scissors their favorite quote and tell why or how it might relate to them.

Sitcom siblings: Using their present families or the ones they grew up in, ask each member to compare his or her family with any TV situation comedy family—past or present.

Idiosyncratic: Write on the chalkboard or an overhead transparency the following statement: "One little thing that really bugs me is. . . ." Members fill in their favorite idiosyncrasies.

Mother of the day: Display the following statement: "If one of the women in the Bible could be my mother, I would want it to be . . . because. . . ." Have members fill in the blanks. This may spark discussion on not knowing enough about women in the Bible to give a good answer.

Change of pace: Have individuals tell what they usually do with their extra change (where they keep it, what they use it for, etc.).

Jingle jangle: Divide the group into clusters of three or four members. Ask them to incorporate an ad for their church into one of their favorite advertising jingles. These will then be performed in front of the larger group.

Jack La . . . who? Ask members to tell what their least favorite form of exercise is.

Scary: Invite members to voice one of their fears and how they deal with it. Have Bible verses that could be comforting in fearful circumstances ready to share with members.

Food, glorious food: Have everyone share his or her favorite and most hated food. Invite members to imagine being needy and the receiver of free food. Discuss what food they would most want to receive and how this relates to food they donate to the needy.

Collecting: Most people collect things at one time or another in their lives. Have your group members tell about one of their collections. If they no longer collect, ask what has happened to the collection.

Notable names: Divide the group into clusters of three or four. Give them five minutes to choose a likely candidate for the strangest name in the Bible. They must find a Scripture reference that includes the name. Share the findings and have the group vote on the strangest name.

Alias "Snookums": Pair up group members. Ask them to tell each other a nickname or pet name they have been called in the past or are presently called. Bring the group back together and let the members introduce their respective partner by his or her pet name or nickname. They may want to give the reason or occasion for this name.

—*Adapted from* How to Be a Christian and Still Enjoy Life *(Gospel Light, 1989)*

Evangelism

67
How to Talk to Strangers

As a child, I was cautioned, "Don't talk to strangers!" But strangers need to hear about Jesus, too. This conviction sent me to malls and fast-food restaurants all around town to disobey my parents' advice. In the process, I learned the following lessons:

Ask questions. I used to approach people with a fixed agenda, armed with a memorized gospel presentation. These information-dumping sessions meant little to my hearers. Now I allow them to "evangelize" me, to educate me about what they believe and why. Once I understand them, I can respond more relevantly. And they are more ready to listen once they feel they've been heard.

Build bridges. I try to arm myself with good conversation starters, then keep alert for natural bridges. Once I asked permission to sit with some girls who were trying to learn to play guitar. I was able to offer my help, and eventually the conversation turned from guitars to God.

Know the basics. I suspect many of us are not excited about sharing the good news because we lack a clear understanding of it. Though gospel presentations like the Bridge to Life can help us cover the key points, we need to have a deeper grasp of God's message for the lost so we are "prepared to give an answer to everyone who asks . . . the reason for the hope that [we] have" (1 Peter 3:15).

Focus. I focus on the person of Christ and a relationship with Him and don't get sidetracked into doctrines and arguments.

Depend on the Holy Spirit. It is God who does the work. I only cooperate with Him. He sensitizes me to the people I approach so I can speak accurately and relevantly.

Demonstrate. When people show curiosity about prayer, I ask if I can pray with them or for them rather than try to explain it. If I share specific verses with them that relate to their circumstances, I show them how to find those verses in the Bible. Whenever possible, I try to leave them with something to go on when they are on their own.

Seek encouragement. Speaking to strangers does not come naturally to me. So I am thankful I have a group of like-minded people to encourage me. We go out together. We pray together. We share our struggles and successes.

—Angeline Koh, Singapore

68
"How Do I Meet My Neighbors?"

You've read oodles of articles and heard scads of sermons about sharing Christ with your neighbors. But you're still stuck at Square One—you have no idea how to meet your neighbors. Try these ideas.

■ *Start simply.* Borrow a cup of sugar or a hammer, ask advice, or offer to help your neighbor move something heavy, change a tire, etc.

■ *Be visible.* Don't hide in your fenced-in back yard. Sit on your porch or stoop. Wash your car in the driveway. Play croquet in your front yard. Make it easier for your neighbors to meet you.

■ *Overplant your garden,* especially if your neighbors don't have gardens. You'll soon have tomatoes to share all up and down your street.

■ *Organize a neighborhood garage sale.* So no one feels pressured, leave flyers on doorsteps, inviting people to call you if they're interested. Plan a potluck dinner after the sale.

■ *Throw a block party.* Hold an Easter egg hunt or go Christmas caroling. Neither of these require a lot of time or expense—dyed eggs (require each family to bring six), coffee, juice, and donuts for the egg hunt; song sheets, hot chocolate or cider, and Christmas cookies (again, make a plate of cookies the price of admission) for the caroling. As with the garage sale, get the word out through flyers.

■ *Organize a neighborhood watch program or baby-sitting cooperative.* Not only will you meet your neighbors, but you'll have natural opportunities for continued, frequent contact.

—*Sue Kline, Colorado Springs, Colorado*

69
Let's Watch a Movie

Movies allow us to explore other cultures and ideas and create an environment for buildings bridges. Why not invite some friends (Christian and nonChristian) over for a movie and discussion? Before you do:

- ■ *View the movie yourself.* You may be looking at it more critically than you did when you only expected to be entertained. Carefully consider what will be most appropriate and effective.
- ■ *Read several reviews.* These will help you discover the movie's themes and feel more comfortable leading the discussion.
- ■ *Prepare questions.* Think of some informal discussion questions to use at the end of the movie.

Be on the lookout for movies with themes of friendship, cultural conflict, or redemption. Here are some possible options:

- ■ On friendship: *The Chosen* (based on the book by Chaim Potok), *Driving Miss Daisy,* and *The Elephant Man.* For discussion, ask "What ingredients are needed to make a friendship?" and "What risks do friendships entail?"
- ■ On cultural conflict: *Iron and Silk, The Gods Must Be Crazy,* and *A Great Wall.* Open your discussion by asking, "Who has visited or lived in another culture?" "How were your experiences similar to or different from those of the characters in this movie?"
- ■ On redemption: *Repentance* (made in the former Soviet Union), *The Story of Qui Ju* (from China), *Tender Mercies, Places in the Heart, The Hiding Place, Chariots of Fire,* and *The Mission.* Discussion questions could probe areas such as faith under fire, personal responsibility, and the power of forgiveness.

Watch for new work by certain directors and writers. Horton Foote wrote the screenplays for *To Kill a Mockingbird, Tender Mercies,* and *A Trip to Bountiful.* Director Peter Wier often combines religious and cross-cultural themes. Woody Allen's *Crimes and Misdemeanors* addresses the topics of sin and guilt.

—*Stacey Bieler, East Lansing, Michigan*

70
They Hope and Pray

Does your faith falter when it comes to your family's salvation? Does the apparent futility make it hard to pray?

I struggled with this, as did four other friends with unsaved family members. We decided to do something about it.

Two years ago we began meeting every other week for two hours solely to pray for our unsaved families. I found early on that I could more easily believe Monica's mother will get saved than Monica could. Likewise, Monica has greater faith for my family's salvation. This teaming up has increased my faith while giving me a proactive involvement in my family's eternal future.

Each meeting begins with a brief update of our families' lives. We created a booklet with color photocopies of the five families and a section entitled "Seed Planting," where we record progress, pitfalls, or glimpses into a family member's spiritual journey. Then we pray over new entries to the book and ask God to draw our loved ones to Him.

Our book also has a section called "The Harvest," where we one day will write in the names of those family members who accept Christ. At the top of the page we scribed, "It is good that a man should both hope and quietly wait for the salvation of the LORD" (Lamentations 3:25).

Since we began meeting, births and marriages have enlarged our family circles, fueling our need to persevere as we "hope and quietly wait" for our families' salvation.

—*Anne Meskey Elhajoui, Colorado Springs, Colorado*

71
Open Home, Open Hearts

God has given many Christians the gift of hospitality. By providing a comfortable atmosphere where Christianity is lived out and where nonChristians feel at ease, homes can be great tools for bringing people to Christ. Try some of these "inreach" ideas in your home.

Dinners for Eight
Dinners for Eight are popular among one church's membership. Eight

people gather for dinner, fellowship, and fun. By including a few nonChristians, new relationships often emerge, leading to invitations to Sunday school classes, worship services, and special church events where the gospel is presented.

Fondue Party
Who can resist chocolate? Invite a group over with the explicit invitation for "Fondue and Discussion of the Christian Faith." Enjoy socializing and dessert. Then have a spiritually mature person make a ten-minute presentation of the relevancy of a relationship with Christ. Open a discussion time for guests to ask questions.

A group of twenty people is best, half nonChristians. Variations on this theme could include evangelistic barbecues, coffee tasting parties, or burrito bars.

Literary Society
Reading groups have gained popularity over the past few years. Begin your own literary society that includes seekers. Gather monthly in a living room to discuss, debate, and dissect a selected reading. Choose Christian and secular authors. Whatever book is chosen, believers can contribute a Christian perspective to the discussion. Encourage an atmosphere of intellectual honesty where believers and nonbelievers alike stretch their thinking.

Youth House
Teenagers love to just hang out. They appreciate homes where they are welcomed, where a wholesome atmosphere provides a place for friendships, and where parents are involved and listen. Maybe your home can be such a place. Not only will you minister to kids, but you will model Christian hospitality for the next generation.

Evangelistic entertaining does not need to be highly formal. Simply ask the Holy Spirit to bless your efforts, enabling nonbelievers to experience the reality of the Christian faith in your home.

—*Keith D. Wright, Kansas City, Missouri*

72
Coffee, Books, and Moms

For more than a year, my friend Jill and I have reached out to other stay-at-home mothers in our neighborhood through a weekly coffee-

and-book-review hour. It has proved both an evangelistic tool and a forum for deeper spiritual growth for those of us who are already Christians. Here are some pointers to help you start and sustain a similar group.

Begin with a core of committed Christians. In this way, the nonChristians can observe the love of Christ among believers, and the Christians can offer valuable input during the discussions.

Frequent "hot spots" for stay-at-home moms. We've met mothers at the park, the library, Little League events, and local fast-food restaurants. When we invite a woman to join our group, we tell her up front that we discuss books about God's role in the parenting process.

Choose the right book. One that already has discussion questions cuts down on preparation time for the leaders. Books we've used with success are *A Mother's Legacy* by Jeanne Hendricks, *What Really Matters at Home* by John and Susan Yates, and *Diapers & Dishes or Pinstripes & Pumps* by Gigi Graham Tchividjian. Some of these we found at the library.

Have plural leadership. We take turns leading the discussion and share in following up group members.

Be open and vulnerable. Our frankness about our struggles has opened doors to fruitful discussion about God as our source of strength and wisdom in all our life roles, including parenting.

Schedule a baby-sitter to come to your home. This helps mothers concentrate on the discussion.

Keep the discussion short. If you go beyond an hour, the mothers get distracted by their children's activities. We leave time before and after the discussion for informal conversations.

Meet weekly. We found this important in building relationships. We meet from September to June, during which time we review three books.

Plan social events. At least once during the school year, we plan an evening of fun, without children! During the summer, we keep in touch through trips to the zoo, park, and pool, and through back-yard potlucks.

Pray. We pray for each woman in the group throughout the week. We also get together fifteen minutes before our meeting to pray. This prayerful focus reminds us that we are doing God's work and He is affecting the results.

—*Tamara J. Boone, Columbus, Ohio*

73
Candid Camera

Here's how you can use video cameras to motivate your group members toward evangelism.

Break into groups of two or three and give each group a video camera. Next, go to a place people hang out (McDonalds, the mall) and ask them if they would like to be on video. Most will agree to being taped.

Ask them these three simple questions:

- Do you believe in God?
- Do you think there is a heaven or a hell?
- What do you think about church?

Collect all the video tapes and edit a fifteen to twenty minute tape. This tape could be incorporated into an evangelistic service or used to encourage small groups to participate in evangelism more regularly.
—*Won Nam, Calgary, Canada*

74
Studying the Bible with New Christians

The illness and death of his father-in-law brought "Biker Bob" to a spiritual turning point. It also brought Bob into our lives and taught us valuable lessons about effective small-group ministry with new Christians.

Lesson 1. Don't expect new Christians to look or act like you do. From the first night I strolled into Bob's house for Bible study, I knew I was in for one of the most unusual small groups I can remember. Two couples sat at the dining room table with big old, dusty family Bibles. The attire was leather jackets and Harley Davidson shirts. Over the next six months we studied almost every verse in the book of Mark, drank gallons of coffee, ate dozens of cookies, and inhaled lungfuls of secondhand smoke.

Part of taking the good news to their turf included no condemnation for habits they had lived with for years. I decided to let the Holy Spirit make the changes He wanted when He wanted.

Lesson 2. *New Christians tell others about their discoveries.* Soon the two original families invited friends, until six others had joined in our discussions.

Lesson 3. *Let new Christians make their own discoveries from Scripture.* Bob and his brother-in-law earned the nickname "Sons of Thunder" for their boisterous outbursts of insight. Bob was elated over every new discovery. He would exclaim, "Wow! This stuff is great. It's giving me goose bumps, man!"

The more we kept quiet, the more the others thought about, and answered, the study-guide questions. Our excitement grew from watching others learn how to study Scripture without relying on the "resident experts" for all the answers.

Bob was especially careful not to evaluate wrong answers. He said, "I just figured I would let them lay their own goose eggs, and after some others gave their answers, the goose eggs would stick out like a sore thumb."

He was right. Some strange interpretations were offered, but without critical comment. People in the group learned to carefully observe what was in Scripture and corrected most strange answers themselves.

Lesson 4. *New Christians are capable of guiding a study, with the proper tools.* At the very first study, I told them they would lead the discussions. I would show them how, then they would take turns asking the questions and reading the passage. They looked surprised but nodded agreement.

I introduced them to the discussion style and gave them a review of our group guidelines. The right tools made a difference, and our new Christian friends became quite good at guiding a lively and fruitful discussion.

Lesson 5. *Veteran Bible students learn new insights along with the new Christians.* One evening Bob said, "The Holy Spirit really doinked me this week," as he smacked his own forehead. What he meant was obvious.

"Doinks" were not reserved for Bible study novices like Bob. One longtime Bible student received her doink when one of the rookies pointed out that we "churched" types resemble Pharisees in some ways. It was a painful but true lesson that our religious rituals can replace our relationship with Christ. One group member exclaimed, "These new Christians keep us on our toes, because they look at Scripture with an open mind."

Our study with new Christians showed us that fresh discoveries are possible even for old-timers of the faith.

—*Clark Cothern, Adrian, Michigan*

75
Reaching the People on Your Street

Are the members of your small group looking for a way to reach out to their neighborhoods? They may want to capitalize on the fact that many people consider themselves religious. Using the same approach as a "block party," Candy Simonson sent out invitations to her neighbors inviting them to her home for a Neighborhood Prayer Party. Candy says, "We informed them that the purpose of this meeting was not only to associate with neighbors surrounding our homes, but to join together in prayer for the protection of our neighborhood and our children.

"First we had refreshments and a time for introductions and sharing about our families. Then each family was encouraged to share a particular need we could all pray for. If they weren't comfortable praying aloud, the leader (or host) prayed.

"This event could be adapted to fit your particular community. A neighborhood picnic, a morning brunch, or serving ice cream and cake may give further incentives to come. This outreach can prove to be an opener for future studies and discussions concerning the Lord."
—*Candy Simonson, Huron, Ohio*

Inviting Children to Church
Have you longed to share the gospel with the children in your neighborhood without offending their parents? One surprisingly simple solution is to invite children, through their parents, to attend the church with you.

You might assume that people who are hostile to Christianity wouldn't let their children attend church, but during the last three years I have taken the children of Moonies, Jews, agnostics, and other nonChristians to services with me. There the children have heard about Jesus Christ and, for those who chose to return, found a family of believers to parent them spiritually.

So get rid of the idea that the parents will automatically say no. Then be alert to every opportunity to invite a child to church.

■ Does your *neighbor* have her hands full with a new baby? Offer to take her older children to church with you, giving Mom a break and the kids some extra attention.

■ Is your *coworker* going through a difficult divorce? Tell him that the children's program at your church can provide emotional support for his child during this difficult time. Is he concerned about his child's choice of friends? Describe the benefits of friendships built within your church's youth group.

■ Is your *unsaved relative* at the end of her marital rope? Offer to take her children to dinner every Wednesday night, then to family activities at church, so she and her husband can have a chance to work on their relationship.

■ Are your children doing something special in church next week—singing in the choir, performing in a play? Encourage them to invite their *friends* to come see them perform. In this way, your child can learn at an early age how important it is to reach out to their unchurched friends.

As you pray for and seek opportunities like those listed above, remember that parents are most likely to say yes if they have already observed love and compassion in the way you live. Begin by being a warm, caring neighbor, coworker, and relative. Parents need to know you genuinely care about them and their children and don't just view them as evangelistic "projects."

—*Barbara Hope Hulford, Philadelphia, Pennsylvania*

76
Hitting the Highways

A Los Angeles church, Eagle Rock Baptist, discovered a unique way to let its light be seen, through California's Adopt-a-Highway program. The church adopted a two-mile roadside stretch along Highway 134. Once a month, a crew of six to eight Eagle Rock members picks up litter along both sides of the highway and on the freeway ramps.

"We have the distinction of having the mile that precedes the dump," says member Marge Durden. "It's a pretty dirty stretch."

Marge and her daughter Janel, age twenty-four, work alongside their pastor and a cross section of members from youths to seniors. The crew begins work at seven A.M. Saturday, and as soon as they finish picking up the litter—usually two to three hours later—they go out for breakfast.

"Sometimes communities tend to think churches are self-serving," says Janel Durden. "We show them we want to be part of the community and that we're willing to give something back. We want people to know we're concerned about them, but also about the environment.

"It's also a way to plant the church's name in people's minds. When they're looking for a church, they'll think of us. They may feel they already know us."

The Saturday work crew is highly visible in their safety gear: bright orange vests with the church's name and logo on the back, hard hats, gloves, and safety glasses. Courtesy signs placed at the beginning and end of the adopted segment publicize the church's participation: "Litter Removal Next Two Miles/Eagle Rock Baptist Church."

"At least four people said they came to our church after seeing the highway signs," says Pastor Rick Mandl. He places the church's Adopt-a-Highway participation in the "broad category of evangelism," and says, "It's a way to touch the unchurched with the message that we're here when they need us."

—*Patricia Ann McNeely, Orlando, Florida*

77
An Investment in Learning

One way your small group can directly impact lives is by setting aside money each month to purchase books, videos, tapes, and other resources to share with others.

Check with your local library about the procedures for donating material. Then select quality Christian videos, books, and books on tape. Your investment can have an ongoing effect in your community.

Another ministry is to provide resources to Christian workers, such as youth pastors, who often operate under tight budget constraints. I have acquired a small collection of videos that I loan to youth workers to use with the kids. Mars Hill Productions (800-580-6479) have produced extremely effective videos geared for teenagers. Vision Video (800-523-0226) carries movies about key figures from church history. And the Adventures in Odyssey audio cassette series from Focus on the Family (719-531-5181) are so good that I get hooked every time my kids listen to them.

Don't overlook a year-round gift of encouragement and inspiration—a magazine subscription (for example, *Discipleship Journal!*). When a small group pools its resources in this way to invest in the lives of others, the dividends far exceed the cost.

—*John Green, Page, Arizona*

78
Caroling and Candy Canes

Does your church hold a cantata or special service to celebrate Christmas? If so, your small group can help spread the word to people who might not otherwise attend a church function during Christmas time. You'll need:

- A plentiful supply of candy canes
- Handmade gift tags
- Tape
- Song sheets
- Enthusiastic carolers

If you can recruit other small groups to participate, you can cover more neighborhoods. If your small group is going it alone, plan to carol in the neighborhood closest to your church.

Schedule your night of caroling a week before your church's Christmas program.

Early in December, purchase enough candy canes to distribute to the homes you visit. Estimate three or four people per household. In lieu of your typical small-group meeting, spend an evening cutting handmade gift tags from red and green construction paper. On one side, write out a verse (perhaps Isaiah 9:6, Luke 2:10-11, or John 3:16). On the other side, write an invitation to your church's Christmas service, giving the essential information plus the church's phone number. (You may want to type the verses and invitations into a computer and print them in bulk. Just cut them to size and glue them to the gift tags.) Tape a gift tag to each candy cane.

While you prepare the candy canes, distribute song sheets of some familiar Christmas carols. You'll only need about six songs since you'll be singing some of the same songs over again as you move throughout the neighborhood. The important thing is to give group members time to refresh their memories of the lyrics since it's hard to read song sheets in the dark! While you're making gift tags, you can rehearse.

After your caroling, meet at a group member's home for hot drinks and cookies and to pray for the people to whom you've given invitations.

—*Sue Kline, Colorado Springs, Colorado*

79
Street Smart Evangelism

In his book *What They Don't Teach You at Harvard Business School: Notes from a Street Smart Executive,* Mark McCormack presented principles for success in the business world. While evangelism should never be viewed as a business, many of McCormack's principles are transferable to the communication of the gospel.

1. *Listen aggressively.* Christians frequently don't take time to hear people's questions. We need to learn to listen. Once we know where someone is hurting, we are in a much better position to speak to his her needs.
2. *Take the edge.* In McCormack's book, "taking the edge" refers to the art of using the facts of the deal to your best advantage. For Christians, this means we must know the message we want to share. Learn several ways to present the gospel so the Holy Spirit can guide you to the most appropriate method for each individual.
3. *Be honest.* Three difficult but helpful phrases, according to McCormack, are "I don't know," "I need help," and "I was wrong." Many unchurched people are skeptical of Christians who appear to have all the answers in a neat little box. They are refreshed and encouraged to find that Christians are real.
4. *Be aware of timing.* One common error in evangelism is missed timing. Some evangelists are so anxious to lead a person to Christ that they press for a decision before the person is ready. Others are so afraid of pushing too hard that they never get around to asking a person to accept Christ. Be sensitive to the Holy Spirit's leading.
5. *Use silence constructively.* Silence is a rare commodity, and it often makes people uncomfortable. But when we let silence enter our conversation, we give the person time to think about our message, and we allow the Holy Spirit to do His work in evangelism—convict the person of his need and of Christ's sufficiency to meet that need.

—*Bradley Price Roderick, Dauphin, Pennsylvania*

Serving

80
Small Groups:
Becoming Salt and Light

God's people have always been called upon to demonstrate their love by meeting the needs of others. The early Christians were instructed to contribute to the needs of the saints (Romans 12:13) and to show hospitality to strangers (Hebrews 13:2). The Church practiced this to such an extent that Luke was able to make this incredible observation of them: "there were no needy persons among them" (Acts 4:34).

A crucial function of small groups in the Church is to provide a vehicle through which Christians can demonstrate their love by meeting the needs of others. Small-group members who want to meet the needs of people in their community will embrace the philosophy of being on call to minister to those needs. They will see themselves as God's resources to needy individuals.

As believers respond to their study of God's Word they will give of themselves to meet someone else's need. Groups can create a resource bank of professional expertise, trade skills, and financial resources.

Caring may be demonstrated in one or more of the following areas: ministering to someone with material needs, comforting someone who is suffering, or counseling someone with a spiritual problem. Here are some ways small groups can minister to others:

- Provide food to *fill the cupboards* of a needy single parent.
- Buy a *round-trip airline ticket* for a disabled person to visit an aging parent.
- Take over the responsibility for the *care of small children* while their mother is hospitalized and recovering from surgery.
- Invest time on a Saturday doing *yard work and painting* for a needy widow.
- *Provide a car* for a missionary during his furlough in the States.

You can be sure that the level of caring in the group has matured when the group members minister not only to each other, but to others outside the group. When a group member says to the group, "My neighbor has a need I think we could meet," and the group responds with a desire to be of service, they are caring the way Jesus cares — with unconditional love.

Works of loving service to those outside the group demonstrate the love of Christ in winsome and attractive ways. This genuine caring provides opportunities to share the good news of salvation as well.

The small group becomes salt and light when it has Christlike influence and impact on its community.

—*Tom Lovejoy, Associate Pastor, FLOCKS ministry, Grace Community Church, Sun Valley, California*

81
Caring Gestures

On your own, read the following checklist and put a check mark next to every way you've expressed care to another person in the past six months.

☐ Sending a card
☐ Providing transportation
☐ Caring for a child
☐ Preparing food
☐ Contributing financial help
☐ Furnishing career assistance
☐ Writing a note
☐ Providing a meal
☐ Giving a hug
☐ Listening actively
☐ Presenting a gift
☐ Shopping for food
☐ Volunteering
☐ Giving a party

☐ Doing manual labor
☐ Holding a hand
☐ Extending hospitality
☐ Making a hospital visit
☐ Providing nursing care
☐ Tutoring
☐ Being present
☐ Offering prayer
☐ Cleaning
☐ Discipling
☐ Making phone calls
☐ Visiting a home
☐ Sewing
☐ Reading

Next, complete the following sentence. "As a result of doing this exercise, I realize that I usually throw ropes to hurting people by. . . ."

Now, as a group, discuss what you have discovered by doing this exercise.

In Ephesians 2:10 we read, "For we are his workmanship, created in Christ Jesus to do good works, which God prepared in advance for us to do." God not only prepares the works, He prepares us to do them.

—*From* Caring Without Wearing *by Carol Travilla (NavPress, 1990), out of print*

82
Accountability-Missions Groups

Accountability-missions groups are more than week-to-week "check-ups" to make sure everyone is serving in some way.

An accountability-missions group is a small group of people who want to take seriously the claims of Jesus Christ upon their lives and want to be involved in daily life ministry.

The focus of the group meeting is to help each other find ways to serve. Some of the questions group members ask each other are: "What is one activity or attitude I believe God wants me to do or have this week?" "What person(s) should I be serving?" "How should I serve?" "How much help will I need?"

In an accountability-missions group, members choose tasks individually through reflection and prayer with the support of the other members: a homemaker shares her desire for a ministry to her children's neighborhood friends, a lawyer discusses his ministry to children involved in the juvenile court system, a couple speaks of their struggle with a handicapped child. Each person shares an area in which he or she feels called to serve God that week.

The following week each member reports how it went—failures, successes, sorrows, joys.

Forming an accountability-missions group provides support for Christian coworkers who desire to have a ministry at the office too. Although each person may interpret God's call somewhat differently, together they can pray, think, confront, and support each other as God's people in that place.

—*From* Service Unlimited, Eight Steps to Constructive Lay Ministry *by Roberta L. Hestenes, reprinted by permission.*

83
Twenty Ways to Encourage a Brother or Sister in Christ

First Thessalonians 5:1-11 tells us that Christ died for us so that we can live together with Him. "Therefore encourage one another and build each other up. . . ."

It is crucial that we encourage our brothers and sisters in our small groups, where we "live together with Him." Here are some specific ways to do so.

- Write an encouraging letter (Paul to Timothy).
- Share how God has dealt with you in your life—your personal testimony of overcoming and growth (Paul's testimony in Acts 22).
- Maintain loyalty in brotherly friendships, not withholding friendship when a brother stumbles or embarrasses you (Joseph and Mary, Paul and the Corinthians).
- Offer your supportive presence, even when you do not understand (the women at the Cross).
- Share specific helpful Scriptures (author of Hebrews to the Hebrew Christians).
- Be an example or model (Paul, as in 2 Corinthians 7:2, 1 Peter 5:3, 1 Timothy 4:12, Philippians 3:17).
- Affirm another person's worth by doing kindness when he hurts (Jesus in Matthew 25—feed the hungry, visit the prisoners, clothe the naked, etc.).
- Show hospitality (entertain—Hebrews 13:2, 1 Peter 4:9).
- Compliment a brother on the progress he makes in the faith (1 Thessalonians 1, 1 Peter 1:22).
- Absorb another person's problems into yourself (pay his debts—Paul with Onesimus; the good Samaritan).
- Rejoice with another in his successes (Acts 5:41).
- Be a cheerleader (offer celebration when the situation looks dim—Paul and Silas in prison).
- Jump in and help someone else actually complete a job (John and Peter with Philip in Samaria).
- Be psychologically available and willing to listen (Paul corresponded with the Corinthians when they needed and asked for his help).

- Stand up for a brother or sister, defending that person when others disparage him or her (Barnabas for Paul).
- Show a gentle, affectionate, concerned, sympathetic attitude (1 Thessalonians 2:7).
- Dialogue, discuss, study together (Paul and the Jerusalem council).
- Give money, food, etc. (Corinthians and Macedonians to brethren in drought).
- Pray (Paul for the Romans).
- Review with a brother or sister the record of God's involvement in our past and present so he or she can get the future into perspective (Paul to the Philippians, and on the shipwreck).

—Source unknown

84
When It Can't Be Fixed — Comfort for the Hurting

What do you say to someone who's hurting, with no solution in sight? What comfort can you offer when no words seem sufficient? Some problems have no real solutions. Children are born with serious handicaps. Businesses fail. Incurable illnesses strike. Having had far more experience with insoluble problems than I would wish, I offer the following suggestions for giving comfort in "impossible" situations.

Be available. Let your friend know you will be there, whenever needed, for as long as needed. Knowing that can itself be an enormous comfort.

Listen. Listen with your ears, your eyes, your whole posture. The gift you have to offer is more often a listening ear than a practical solution.

Offer specific, practical help. Can you accompany your friend to a meeting with the doctor, as moral support? Can you run an errand, mow a lawn, or baby-sit a child long enough to allow your friend a nap or time to cry? Ask what's needed most.

Organize support. Volunteer to coordinate people who will baby-sit, make meals, do laundry, housework, etc.

Inquire about finances. If this crisis results in lost wages, additional medical bills, and other financial burdens, ask tactfully but directly if the family is going to be able to manage. If not, could the church pay a month's rent? The phone bill? Cover car repairs? Send over several bags of groceries?

Assist with red tape. The number of doctors, insurance companies, social organizations, etc., that one has to deal with in certain situations can be absolutely overwhelming. Could someone else call the doctor or insurance company and straighten out the bill? Offer to be a buffer between your friends and these bureaucracies.

Include your friends in the normal activities of life. When a problem is long-term, you can't just put life on hold till it's over. Invite the children to a birthday party, movie, or dinner at McDonald's. Have your friends over for a meal or arrange a quiet evening alone for husband and wife.

Pray and let your friend know you are praying. Ask for prayer requests, too.

Keep at it. Often support is offered in abundance in the first days following a crisis but slows to a trickle in the weeks, months, and years that follow, when discouragement and exhaustion may make support all the more necessary.

—*Barbara Hope Hulford, Philadelphia, Pennsylvania*

85
Hospitality to Go

Have you ever considered that meaningful hospitality doesn't have to take place in the giver's home? In fact, in certain situations, meeting on our friends' turf may be more helpful than inviting them to ours. Think about these ideas the next time you want to pack your hospitality to go.

■ When a friend is convalescing, call and ask if you can share your lunch with him or her. Then load a picnic basket with a thermos of soup and some sandwiches or salad.

■ If a family you know is going through an extended period of difficulty—maybe the wife is expecting a rough pregnancy, or they have just brought an elderly parent into their home—consider doubling your recipes and freezing the extra meals whenever you can. Deliver them regularly, making sure everything is in disposable containers and clearly marked with directions for heating and serving.

■ When a family first brings foster children (or a new or adopted baby) into their home, they're busy trying to get everyone used to a new routine, and may hesitate to go out very much. Ask if you can deliver a meal and meet their new family member. Take along a game for the kids, then stay awhile and play it with them.

■ When someone you know is spending long hours at the hospital with a seriously ill loved one, take a couple of bag lunches when you visit. You friend may appreciate a break from lonely trips to the hospital cafeteria.

■ Just about anyone enjoys a picnic. Some sunny day, pack everything you'll need for a picnic lunch, then invite someone to join you at the park. On a Sunday after church, this could be a great way to welcome the new family that has started coming to your church.

—*Cindy Hyle Bezek, Evansville, Indiana*

86
Mercy In a Minute

When I think of mercy, I think of Mother Teresa, who shows love to the neediest of the needy. Or my friend Thelma, who tells prostitutes in Manila about Jesus' love. Or Phyllis, who chooses to teach in the inner city when she could make more money and have fewer hassles at a safe suburban school.

Few of us will perform such heroic acts of mercy, but all of us can practice mercy (compassion in action) in small ways. For example:

■ The next time someone shares a hurt with you, don't just say, "I'll pray for you." Take them aside right then and pray for them.

■ Whenever you write a check to that missionary you support, take time to write a newsy postcard. Your money is important, but so is your caring.

■ Inquire at a local nursing home about which patients never receive visitors. Visit once a month. Take along a book of short stories, a magazine, or a newspaper, and read to them.

■ The next time a friend visits you because she needs to talk, turn on the answering machine and ignore the phone. Your uninterrupted attentions says, "You're important to me."

■ While you're raking your leaves, rake your neighbor's as well. You might be easing the pressure of an overwhelming do-list.

■ Is a friend's car out of commission? Take her with you for a morning of running errands (run *her* errands, not just yours!), then treat her to lunch. When circumstances are working against us, it's nice to know people are "for us."

■ Watch for people at church who sit alone, stand alone after the service, or otherwise look lonely. Introduce yourself. Make a double date to meet them for coffee and donuts on the following Sunday.

—Sue Kline, Colorado Springs, Colorado

87
Help for the Homeless

From the fall 1994 issue of *Leadership* come two ideas for serving the homeless. They could become ministries of your entire congregation, your Sunday school class, your neighborhood association, etc. Be creative in adapting these ideas to fit your group and your community.

At All Saints' Episcopal Church in Boise, church members bring specific items to donate to homeless shelters. The monthly schedule looks like this:

January	toothpaste/toothbrushes
February	cold and flu remedies
March	laundry soap and bleach
April	baby items
May	T-shirts
June	personal hygiene items
July	sheets and towels
August	school supplies
September	socks
October	mittens and gloves
November	coats and sweaters
December	hot-drink mixes/juices

At a San Diego church, members assembled lunch bags for the homeless with enough food for one day. The contents:

☐ two breakfast bars
☐ two pop-top cans of tuna

☐ two pop-top cans of fruit
☐ a small tube of toothpaste
☐ a small bar of soap
☐ a plastic fork and spoon
☐ three boxed juices
☐ two granola bars
☐ a tooth brush
☐ a napkin
☐ a New Testament
☐ a five-dollar bill
☐ a letter from the congregation

—From the fall 1994 issue of Leadership

88
Your Community Needs You

Volunteer organizations are hungry for people who will step in and serve their community. Whether you're feeding the hungry, enhancing you town's culture, or serving the local school, you are demonstrating that you care about the people around you. This is a message worth communicating in an age when many communities view Christians as enemies who want to control how their communities are run. Here are some ways to serve:

- Offer to volunteer at the local library. Libraries often need board members, volunteers to read during preschool programs, grant writers, or book shelvers.
- Begin a program for moms at home. Many mothers become isolated when they decide to stay home, and social activities that welcome parent and child are a genuine service to families.
- Run for local office, or ask to be appointed to a local board such as planning or zoning. Get involved with special-events planning for your town or city.
- Join a service group such as Rotary, Lions, or Sertoma. Attend chamber of commerce meetings.
- Become an officer in the local parent-teacher organization, ask to be appointed to the school's budget or planning committee, or run for school board.

- Get your church to produce a newsletter that not only includes events of your church but concerns of the community as well. Distribute it at local secular outlets.
- Make a list of volunteer opportunities in your community and distribute it to your Christian friends.

—*Michele McFee, Bainbridge, New York*

89
Six Ways to Serve
Your Community

Project warmth. Collect blankets, coats, and other warm clothing for the homeless. One group advertises their annual "blanket run" in the church newsletter and receives several truckloads of donated items. They also approach area businesses for monetary donations to buy rain ponchos and socks (the most requested items). Deliver your bounty to local homeless shelters and soup kitchens for distribution.

Graffiti be gone. Gather buckets, scrub brushes, sandpaper, hoses, etc. and throw a graffiti clean-up party. Concentrate on a single area and you can achieve tangible results in one day.

Urban garden. Help urban dwellers turn an abandoned city lot into a garden by providing seeds, tools, and muscle. Begin by checking with City Hall in case special permits are required. Then set a time to plant the garden, alongside other neighborhood residents. As you tend the garden all summer, relationships will grow along with the plants.

Prettify a park. Is there a neglected park in your neighborhood? Get permission from the appropriate local agency, then roll up your sleeves. You'll need trash bags, work gloves, brooms, and gardening implements. Bring large pieces of screen to sift broken glass, gum, and dangerous objects from sandboxes. You may also need tools for repairing fences. Paint hopscotch and foursquare courts on the asphalt. Ask local businesses to donate fresh sand or tan bark.

Expect plenty of onlookers. Perhaps you could invite the curious to a cookout at the park to celebrate its restoration.

Treating without the tricks. Instead of collecting treats at Halloween, distribute them. One small group dressed in amusing (but nonscary) costumes and distributed sweets at a children's hospital (check with the hospital first). This group was able to pray with some of the children's parents, providing hope and encouragement.

Gleanings. Farms and orchards in your area may allow you to collect leftover fruit and vegetables for distribution to food ministries. Groups who've done this are often amazed at the amount of food they can collect in a day.

—*Keith D. Wright, Kansas City, Missouri*

90
Show a Person with AIDS You Care

AIDS is an indiscriminate killer. It afflicts young and old, rich and poor, white and black, homosexual and heterosexual, Christian and nonChristian. Here are some practical things you can do to show Christ's love to people with AIDS.

■ *Visit them in the hospital or in their homes.* Many people afflicted with AIDS have been abandoned by their families and friends, and they're desperate for personal contact. Research indicates that the AIDS virus is transmitted only through a significant exchange of blood or fluids, so don't let unfounded fears keep you from touching and hugging people who are aching to feel Christ's love.

■ *Hate the sin, love the sinner.* People who contracted AIDS through homosexual behavior or drug abuse will expect you to blame and judge them. Surprise them with concern and compassion.

■ *Form a group to help with meals or home maintenance.* As AIDS progresses, the victim's strength diminishes. A hot meal or help with the housework can visibly express Christ's love.

■ *Assist financially.* Most AIDS victims soon grow too sick to work, if they don't lose their jobs before then. That means dwindling incomes and mounting medical bills. Any financial help Christians can provide will go a long way in showing a person with AIDS that God cares.

■ *Pray with them.* Your prayers will encourage and comfort those with AIDS. They can also provide tangible physical and emotional help for AIDS sufferers.

—*Steve Arterburn, Laguna Beach, California*

91
An Application Bible Study on Servanthood

SCRIPTURE
Look up each of these references and respond to the questions that follow: Matthew 18:1-5, 20:25-28, 23:1-12; Mark 9:33-37, 10:35-44; Luke 9:23-25,46-49, 22:24-27; John 13:12-17; Philippians 2:5-11.

QUESTIONS
1. Forgetting our usual marks of leadership, if you were to make a list of people who serve selflessly, who would be on that list?
2. From the Scriptures above, you could get a list of servanthood traits that would look like this: servant, example, humble, child, younger, least, last, no force, no blind ambition, no reputation, human, obedient unto death. In which of these do you feel strongest and in which do you feel weakest?
3. For each of the other members of the group, state in which of these traits you think he or she is strongest.
4. If you were to "wash someone's feet" who would you go to and what would you do for him or her?

—*Gayle D. Erwin, reprinted from a booklet of Servant Quarters, West Covina, California*

92
Eight Ways to Serve Your Local School

Confrontations between Christians and public school systems are often in the news. We admire those courageous souls who face the issues head-on. But what if we aren't the confrontational type? Is there anything we can do to influence our public schools for the good?

We can serve. By His own testimony, Jesus came not as a military conqueror, not as a political leader, not as a celebrity, but as a servant. And as a servant, He has changed countless lives over many centuries.

Worldwide Challenge (January/February 1994) lists ways you can influence your local school through serving.

- Pray for administrators, teachers, students, and parents by name. *Mothers Who Care* is a group committed to praying for children, schools, and communities. For information about them, write to Mothers Who Care, 100 Sunport Lane, Dept. 2600, Orlando, FL 32809.
- Volunteer in the school setting to allow others to see Christ in you. Tutor, decorate classrooms at the start of the semester, coach, help in the office or library, chaperone field trips, be a "room mother."
- Write letters to the administration, praising them for things they are doing well or for their strong moral values. Also write to express concerns or observations.
- Invest your prayers or finances in someone with a ministry to students or faculty. Ask them if there are practical ways you can serve them and their ministry.
- Bring coffee or donuts to the teachers' lounge along with a thank-you note to encourage the educators.
- Help your children reach out to classmates. Teach them how to communicate their faith in Christ. Help them incorporate what they believe into their school projects and speeches.
- Open your home to gatherings for students, teachers, or administrators. Youth workers often need a place to hold meetings and would be encouraged to have your support.
- Donate books to the school library.

—Worldwide Challenge Magazine

Missions

93
Making Missionary Prayer a Habit

A recent missionary newsletter from a difficult country said, "We ran out of emotional energy and felt we just couldn't handle any more. If people back home stop praying, we're not going to make it." Your prayers sustain missionaries.

One practical way to approach praying for your missionaries is to devote each day of the week to a specific area of their lives. Aim for six days a week. If you manage seven, you'll feel the satisfaction of going beyond your goal.

Monday: Inner life and growth. For spiritual disciplines. For confidence in God's sovereignty when things go wrong. For God's mighty touch in relieving stress.

Tuesday: Relationships. With their partner and children, with coworkers, with unbelievers, and with authorities in the country.

Wednesday: Special needs in a foreign culture. Mastering the language. Defense against loneliness, homesickness, frustration. Insights into how to communicate the truth. God's sovereign working in government decisions and politics.

Thursday: Ministry. For Christ to be manifested through their lives day by day. For God to empower them for their work. For His blessing on their evangelism, discipling, and church responsibilities. For their specific area of service, such as administration, nursing, doctoring.

Friday: The nitty-gritty. Physical health. Financial provision. Coping with red tape. Wise use of time. For strength and faith in trials. That they will take adequate time for exercise, relaxation, sports, hobbies, vacation.

Saturday: Victory. Against Satan as he seeks to keep people blinded to the gospel and thwart the growth of believers.

Praying for missions is not a fringe activity from God's point of view. By praying you can play a major role in God's great purposes. Prayer gives you the opportunity to make a vast difference in this world. Your prayers are vital.

—*Ruth Myers, condensed from* World Disciple *(winter 1994), used with permission*

94
Setting Up Prayer Groups for Missions

A few years ago, God led South Evangelical Presbyterian Fellowship in Denver, Colorado, to expand its idea of missions beyond writing letters and sending money. The church began to see missions as its reason for existence, not just part of its program.

As the church's perspective on missions broadened, church members saw the necessity of training people for missions and *praying faithfully for them.* Here are some of their ideas for setting up successful prayer groups to support the missions of the church in the community and abroad.

Prayer groups usually begin in one of two ways: either a long- or short-term missionary asks a group of people to support him or her in prayer, or one person feels led to pray for a specific ministry or mission in some area of the world and organizes a group. At South Evangeical Presbyterian Fellowship, each short-term missionary is asked to recruit ten people to pray for him during the course of his mission. If each of the ten people is in a different small group, the missionary could conceivably have ten groups committed to praying for him!

However, if one individual feels the burden to pray for missions, he or she faces the task of setting up a group that meets specifically for prayer as opposed to a group that meets for another purpose (such as Bible study or fellowship) and is committed to praying for a missionary.

The most successful of these groups are the ones that are targeted toward a specific area of the world (e.g., Hindu world, Moslem world). The benefits of this kind of group are fourfold:

1. The group can focus clearly on what is going on in a given area and pray for its specific needs.
2. Members will often join the group because they have a special interest in praying for that area. Thus the group maintains a high level of interest and commitment.
3. This kind of prayer group can serve as encouragement to group members who might be considering missionary work themselves. As they pray for that mission, they might get a clearer sense of the Lord's leading.
4. Some members of the group might be praying for and finan-

cially supporting a missionary. Their involvement in a group of this kind will help them to understand their friend's situation and will enhance their personal prayers for him or her.

Each member of the group should be responsible for at least one meeting and make a presentation on some aspect of the area the group is praying for. Information is a key to a sustained level of interest and effectiveness in a prayer group. And because each member is responsible to lead one meeting, he has a sense of ownership in the group which is closely tied to the prayer requests.

—*Navigator staff*

95
A Care Package They'll Crave

During six years of cross-cultural ministry in Asia, I learned through happy experience what makes a great care package.

Size is immaterial. One of my favorite care packages was a chocolate candy bar tucked inside a letter. It was destroyed by the Manila heat, but no less cherished. Less fragile ideas include:

- Taped sermons (music to the ears of those who listen to sermons delivered in another language)
- Music cassettes, sheet music
- Holiday decorations (not all countries celebrate the same holidays as those in the U.S.)
- Packaged food—chili seasoning, jello, instant soups, muffin mixes, chewing gum, tea bags
- Reminders of home—a souvenir T-shirt, a scenic calendar, a home-team baseball cap
- Comic strips and editorial cartoons from the local newspaper
- Collections of greeting cards
- Simple toys like balsa-wood airplanes, paper dolls, stickers, puzzles
- Photos
- Recipes
- Cosmetics

- Magazines
- Adult and children's books
- Hobby supplies
- Plastic containers and "zippered" plastic bags
- Travel-sized toiletries
- *Number one most coveted care package item:* chocolate chips

Your small group can adopt a missionary family to send care packages and become one of their most treasured connections to home.
—*Sue Kline, Colorado Springs, Colorado*

96
A Long-Distance Shower

Looking for a fun, practical way to minister to missionaries? The next time a missionary couple announces they're going to have a baby, host a long-distance baby shower for them.

First, if they are living overseas, make sure they can safely and economically receive packages. In some countries, fees to "liberate" a parcel are far higher than its value.

Your next step is to plan the baby shower just as you would if the parents-to-be were present. Ask invitees to bring a note of encouragement and a wrapped gift. (Keep in mind that postage is calculated according to weight. This can get astronomical when shipping overseas.) Take plenty of snapshots to enclose with the gifts.

"You'll never know how timely such a shower was for us," says one former missionary couple. "We weren't making much money as church planters in Arizona. One Sunday we tithed, knowing the money could have been used to buy baby things. The very next day we received a huge box from people we'd never met. We sat on our living room floor and cried as we opened gift after gift for our new baby."
—*Clark Cothern, Adrian, Michigan*

97
An Evening in Mingouwee

To heighten missions awareness and interest, plan a small-group or family event in which you "visit" another country. Select a country where one of your church-supported missionaries serves, ideally a missionary you already know personally or who will be visiting your area on furlough. You will need:

From the Missionary
- A recipe for a typical meal from the chosen country
- An explanation of any mealtime customs that differ from those in the United States
- The words and pronunciation for "help yourself," "please," "thank you," and "that was very good"
- Prayer requests for the missionary's family and ministry
- A family photo and snapshot or postcards of the missionary's country, ministry, and daily life

For the Evening
- Decorations such as a country flag, streamers in the colors of the flag, curios, a map, or travel posters
- A meal prepared and served according to the culture
- Information about the country, obtained from encyclopedias, atlases, travel books, and *Operation World,* copied onto place cards or made into a quiz
- Index cards on which foreign phrases are written out for people to practice during the meal
- Copies of prayer requests for your "adopted" missionary and country, which you pray over as a group at evening's end
- Camcorder, tape recorder, or camera for recording the event
- Stationery

To Send the Missionary
- A copy of the video or tape that you made with personal greetings from the group. (Find out beforehand if your missionary can receive parcels like this without cost or hassles.)
- If you didn't have access to a camcorder, newsy letters from group members and snapshots of the evening.

—*Sharon Fleming, Bogota, Colombia*

98
Reach Out to a Refugee

Bosnia. Croatia. Cuba. These are some of the places in today's headlines, and associated with each of them is the word *refugees*.

A refugee has been forced to flee his homeland because of racial, religious, or political persecution. As of 1993, there were over 18 million worldwide. Each year, about 130,000 settle in the United States. Some may be settling in your town or city.

Refugees arrive empty-handed, forced to start all over again. They need help learning their way around, they need essentials like food and clothing, and they need friends.

Through Exodus World Service, you can mobilize your church to serve refugees. Exodus has designed three ministry projects which require different levels of time and financial investment. Their "Welcome to America!" project provides a refugee family with basic household items and a month's supply of food staples. This makes a great project for a small group, Sunday school class, youth group, or vacation Bible school. After collecting all the donated items, you deliver them to a newly arrived refugee family.

A larger-scale program helps a church sponsor a refugee family by providing the refugees with food, clothing, housing, and furnishings; orienting them to life in America; and helping them find jobs.

The "Bethlehem Inn" project helps your family host a refugee family in your home for their first week in America.

For each of these projects, Exodus provides inexpensive ($2) kits that walk you through every detail. You can also request their regular newsletter, *Exodus Network News,* which tells you how others are reaching out to refugees. It's a great idea source.

If you'd like to meet and serve refugees in your area but don't know where to start, get in touch with Exodus World Service, P.O. Box 620, Itasca, IL 60143-0620, phone (708)307-1400.

—*Sue Kline, Colorado Springs, Colorado*

99
Growing Missions-Minded Children

It's never too soon to instill a vision and heart for the world in your children. Here are some ideas to get you started.

- Display the world in your home. One family has a shower curtain with a map of the world on it. Another family hung a world map by their kitchen table and framed it with pictures of missionaries they know. There are globe-imprinted beach balls, key rings, mugs, etc. The point: Your children learn there is a big world out there beyond their home town.
- If your church supports missionaries, find out which ones have children the same ages as yours. Have your kids make birthday, Christmas, and Easter cards for their "adopted" missionary kids. Make a cassette tape in which your children tell about themselves: favorite songs, foods, sports, etc. Enclose a blank tape so the missionary kids can do the same.
- Read missionary biographies. These will teach, inspire, and impress your children with how God uses ordinary people in extraordinary ways.
- Regularly rent travel videos and learn about new places.
- When missionaries visit your church, invite them for lunch or dinner.
- Befriend an international student or family. Ask about their favorite national holiday, then celebrate it with them.
- Sponsor a child through a relief organization. Post the child's picture prominently. Make prayer for your sponsored child a daily habit—perhaps before eating breakfast together.
- Buy *You Can Change the World* by Jill Johnstone. This is a children's version of *Operation World* that features twenty-six countries and twenty-six people groups, so praying for a section a week will take you through the year.

—*Virginia Benson, Baltimore, Maryland*

100
Wanted:
Christian Professionals

Your professional skills may be your passport to world missions. Consider the following avenues for short-term mission service.

Physicians, Dentists, and Nurses

The Christian Medical and Dental Society organizes worldwide outreaches through short-term clinics that care for impoverished people in Jesus' name. By calling (615)844-1000, you can obtain a complete list of upcoming clinics.

A top medical researcher and his wife (a nurse) established a research facility in an Islamic country. They've built friendships with Muslims and enjoyed many natural opportunities to share Christ with other professionals employed by their clinic.

Teachers

During his summer break, a teacher can train other teachers, organize libraries, and teach specialty courses in one of the many schools run by mission organizations. On a short-term trip to Belize, we held a vacation Bible school in a mission's classrooms. Some teachers on our team noticed how outdated the textbooks on the shelves were, and later secured surplus textbooks and school supplies to send to the mission school.

Opportunities for teaching English also abound and are particularly effective avenues into closed countries.

Accountants

Many mission agencies need accountants to conduct internal audits, establish sound fiscal procedures, and ensure conformity to tax laws. One accountant travels to Papua New Guinea each year after tax season to help bring a Wycliffe field office into compliance with the mission's high standards. He brings not just his expertise but also a ministry of encouragement.

Counselors

Cross-cultural ministry takes its toll on missionaries and their families. It also separates them from all the resources of the counseling profession.

Counselors who are willing to travel, scripturally grounded, and sensitive to cross-cultural issues provide a greatly needed service to the missions community.

Pastors
A pastor whose congregation encourages him to participate in cross-cultural ministry reaps the personal benefits of an expanded vision while also bringing encouragement and spiritual vitality to the missionaries he meets.

Attorneys
A growing number of cross-cultural missionaries are tentmakers who practice their professions overseas. They need various legal services to help them secure visas, establish international corporations, and manage financial assets for their businesses. Christian lawyers who offer these services pro bono make a global impact.

MAKING CONNECTIONS
InterCristo, a Christian placement service, matches 215 professions with 20,000 mission opportunities around the globe. Call (800)231-7740 for an application and inventory of needed skills and abilities. InterCristo charges a fee (currently $45) for this computer-processed application and sends you four customized reports of mission possibilities.
—*Keith D. Wright, Kansas City, Missouri*

101
Going Global Without Risk

So you're not ready to get on a jet to Timbuktu or Taganatuan? In *How to Be a World-class Christian*, Paul Borthwick suggests some low- and no-risk activities that can help create a more global environment in your home or with your group.

- Host a missionary and hear firsthand about life in a foreign culture.
- Write to missionaries.
- Host an international student for dinner.
- House an exchange student.

■ Attend cultural events in ethnic neighborhoods.

■ Eat at an international restaurant. (For some, eating Thai food is a very high-risk venture!)

■ Keep prayer cards at the dinner table and pray for a missionary at each evening meal.

■ Support an international project or a child overseas. Involve the youngest family members through contributions of pennies, nickels, and dimes.

■ Take a vacation with a purpose. Help at a missions headquarters. Serve in a vacation Bible school in an ethnic church.

■ Buy a global-learning game and grow in your knowledge of geography.

■ Rent videos about other parts of the world.

—*From* How to Be a World-class Christian *by Paul Borthwick, Lexington, Massachusetts, Victor (1991)*